Nigerian Female Writers
A Critical Perspective

Nigerian Female Writers
A Critical Perspective

Edited by

Henrietta C. Otokunefor

and

Obiageli C. Nwodo

MALTHOUSE PRESS LIMITED

Malthouse Press Limited,
8, Amore Street,
Off Toyin Street, Ikeja
P.O. Box 8917,
Lagos.

Associated Company
Malthouse Publishing Ltd.,
19A Paradise Street,
Oxford, OX1 1LD, UK.

First Published 1989

ISBN 978 2601 09 8

Typeset in Lagos by Fena Typesetters and Graphics Ltd.

Dedication

TO THE NIGERIAN FEMALE WRITERS WHO DARE TO
"CHALLENGE THE DOMINANT PARADIGM"

Contents

List of Contributors

Dr Funso Aiyejina
Department of Literature in English
Obafemi Awolowo University
Ile-Ife

Mr Ayo Akinwale
Department of Performing Arts
Faculty of Arts
University of Ilorin

Dr Chidi Amuta
Department of English Studies
Faculty of Humanities
University of Port Harcourt
Port Harcourt

Dr (Mrs) Helen Chukwuma
Department of English Studies
Faculty of Humanities
University of Port Harcourt

Professor W.F. Feuser
Department of Foreign Languages and Literatures
University of Port Harcourt
Port Harcourt

Professor Chidi Ikonne
Department of English and Literary Studies
University of Calabar

Mr Seiyifa Koroye
Department of English Studies
Faculty of Humanities
University of Port Harcourt
Port Harcourt

Dr Obi Maduakor
Department of English Studies
Faculty of Arts
University of Nigeria
Nsukka

Dr (Mrs) Yemi Mojola
Department of Modern European Languages
Obafemi Awolowo University
Ile-Ife

Professor Charles Nnolim
Department of English Studies
Faculty of Humanities
University of Port Harcourt
Port Harcourt

Mrs Obiageli C. Nwodo
The Library
University of Port Harcourt
Port Harcourt

Dr Olu Obafemi
Department of English
University of Ilorin

Dr (Mrs) Emelia Aseme Oko
Department of English and Literary Studies
University of Calabar

Dr (Mrs) Juliet I. Okonkwo
Department of English
Faculty of Arts
University of Nigeria
Nsukka

Mrs Henrietta C. Otokunefor
The Library
University of Port Harcourt
Port Harcourt

Preface

There is a current dearth of literary materials on Nigerian female writers. It is pertinent to mention however two readily available titles in the market; namely *Women Writers in Black Africa* (Lloyd Brown, 1981) and *Female Novelists of Modern Africa* (Oladele Taiwo, 1984). These works treat African female writers in general laying emphasis on the major authors with little or no room for the others, thus creating the impression that Nigerian female writers are limited to the few established hands such as Flora Nwapa, Buchi Emecheta and Adaora Ulasi.

Chikwenye Okonjo Ogunyemi in her write-up in *The Guardian* (Lagos) of 25 May 1985 titled "Women and Nigerian literature" criticized Nigerian literature as being "Phallic dominated with male writers and critics dealing almost exclusively with male characters and concerns naturally aimed at a predominantly male audience,". In a similar vein, Mabel Segun in her article in *The Guardian* of 13 June 1983 titled "The Literary Contribution of the Nigerian Female Writers" lamented the lack of publicity given to the Nigerian female writers. To correct this imbalance she called for studies that would enhance the image of the Nigerian female writers in order to bring them into the limelight of the Nigerian literary scene. This she believes will encourage more women to write.

Nigerian Female Writers: A Critical Perspective is a timely response to that call. This work has thrown some light on a number of relatively unknown female writers who, in our own opinion, have contributed immensely in their various areas, to the development of Nigerian literature.

Our aim is to bring into focus the literary contribution of all Nigerian female writers up to the present. What we have been able to put together, however, fell short of our lofty expectations largely due to the unavailability of the published works of some of our authors, not even from the authors themselves, in some case. For this group of writers like Anne Akpabot, Rose Anizoba, Anji Ossai etc. only their biographies and/or bibliographies have been included here. Another major setback was the lack of response from some female writers. These were eventually left out of this maiden edition.

The writers have been grouped into four broad categories, namely, the Novelists, the Dramatists, the Poets and the Children Literature Writers. The treatment given each writer includes a short biography; a list of her publications; works about her and a critical analysis of her works.

In carrying out this project we were immensely encouraged by the thoughtful and gracious assistance from Professor C.E. Nnolim,

Dr. C.N. Amuta, Mr. S. Koroye and Mrs. M.D. Segun. We are grateful to the female writers whose timely response persuaded us not to give up midway. We are deeply indebted to our critics who have made this work possible.

Finally, we would like to thank our husbands and children for their encouragement and moral support; and for bearing those endless hours of our absence with graciousness and understanding.

Henrietta Otokunefor
and
Obiageli Nwodo

Port Harcourt,
January 1987

I
The Novelists

Chapter 1

Positivism and the Female Crisis: The Novels of Buchi Emecheta

Dr (Mrs) Helen Chukwuma

The spectrum of modern African writing is given a wider dimension by the novels of Buchi Emecheta. This is a most welcome phenomenon primarily because it has filled the gaping gender gap between male and female characterization, and shown the other side of the coin. The rural, back-house, timid, subservient, lack-lustre woman has been replaced by her modern counterpart, a full-rounder human being, rotational, individualistic and assertive, fighting for, claiming and keeping her own.

Formerly, female characters' trained ambition revolved round marriage and procreation. Her other female obligations ranged further to cooking the family meals, honouring her husband's bed, on invitation; and other times merging with the home environment peacefully. Hence Akubue's customary response to a complimentary question about his family is "They are quiet".[1] In the city novels of Cyprian Ekwensi, characteristically a woman's individuality is asserted only through prostitution.[2] This appears to be the only way of bursting the system of male domination within the marriage institution. And Buchi makes Adaku break her matrimonial shackles in *Joys of Motherhood*, also through prostitution. In both institutions, marriage and prostitution, man is still dominant, the difference being that in the latter only, the female calls the tune.

It is in the background of such female characterization seen in the novels of Chinua Achebe, *Things Fall Apart* (1957), *Arrow of God* (1964) and Elechi Amadi, *The Concubine* (1966), based on our past culture that Buchi Emecheta emerges as a welcome diversion from the canon. The female character has emerged from her cocoon, basking free to a mixed reception of surprise and wonder. Where was she all the while when her mates were sold away to domestic slavery, when they were given away as child-brides to aged husbands of parental choice; when they were denied the opportunity of school or any exposure? When they were deemed outcasts because they were not virgin brides and when after marriage they were victimised for infertility and derided for fecundity of the wrong sex? The answer is simple, the emancipated female was not born then. In Buchi Emecheta, the African female character, the essential female has just emerged.

This essay traces the developmental features of Buchi Emecheta's feminism as seen in her portrayal of female characters from the slave girl prototype to the career mother and single fulfilled woman. It is important in this regard to see Emecheta's technique in pitching her characters in familiar real life situations showing their unique reactions to the *status quo*. Her stance which is positivistic, will be examined later in the essay.

Theme

Buchi Emecheta's central theme in almost all her novels[3] is woman, the feminine gender of the species of *Homo sapiens*. The handicap of the female is natal, just by being born a female child. In *Second Class Citizen*, this point is aptly demonstrated in the character of the protagonist, Adah. "She was a girl who arrived when everyone was expecting and predicting a boy. So, since she was such a disappointment to her parents, to her immediate family, to her tribe, nobody thought of recording her birth. She was so insignificant."[4] Emecheta remarks on Akunna's birth, the first issue of the imbalanced union between Ezekiel Odia and Ma Blackie — "Akunna knew that she was too insignificant to be regarded as a blessing to this unfortunate marriage. Not only was she a girl but she was much too thin for the approval of her parents, who would rather have a strong plump little girl for a daughter."[5] And when it comes to schooling, Adah though older is dropped in preference for her junior brother characteristically called Boy. Emecheta stresses this point of inequality of opportunity between the sexes and the conscious, rationalised effort to subsume the female for the upliftment of the male as the heir.

This theme of economic exploitation and denial of opportunity of the female for the expressed benefit of the male is dominant in Emecheta's novels. Two of her novels explore this theme in great depth. *The Bride Price* (1976) and *The Slave Girl* (1977) show the economic value of women as analagous to chattels of trade and property for sale. Thus a girl's worth as a human being is reduced to the economic level and everything depends on it: her parents, sustenance, payment of her brother's fees, rehabilitation of other members of the extended family.

Akunna, the female protagonist of *The Bride Price*, carries this economic misnomer in her name, which means "father's wealth", because the "only consolation he could count on from her would be her bride price".[6] The great irony of the bride price in Emecheta's novels is that the expected benefits are never realised. Akunna's bride price is not paid and in *Second Class Citizen* Adah's bride price of five hundred pounds is never paid either, to the chagrin of her family. Adah's case is particularly painful because she is an educated female and so understandably would fetch more money. The bride price is central to the marriage transaction, but Emecheta no doubt over-emphasises its economic merit. Ibuzo is not part of the premium on the human than material worth of the female. Rather, the point of an intimidating marriage system is at issue not the monetary gains of the bride price though that helps out families. The bride price still remains a token.

Ogbanje Ojebeta is, unlike other female protagonists, a wanted child, the only surviving female child in a family of two sons. This cherished position with its lavish pampering is soon to give way to the extremity of domestic slavery. Okolie her brother, lacking money and means, sells her to Ma Palagada for eight pounds. She thus supplies the money he direly needs to equip himself for their coming of age dance as the chief dancer of the Uloko group.

The economic exploitation does not end in saleability through the bride price or in downright slavery. In *Second Class Citizen,* Adah who nurtures a dream of going abroad, works and saves up enough money for herself, her husband and children to travel. She finds rather that she is to stay back in Nigeria saddled with the responsi-bility of paying for Francis, looking after herself and her children, her parents-in-law and paying her sister-in-law's fees.[7]

Emecheta's feministic stance is seen in the females' reactions to these situations. Her characters adopt a positivistic view in crisis, and do not just fold their arms in tears and self-pity. Rather, they think, plan, execute and concretize. Through this maze of self-assertion, the female individualism and personality shows, she appears in another light, as a person capable of taking and effecting decisions. Thus as Adah is frustrated in her plans to travel abroad she changes her tactics and instead of direct confrontation and antagonism, a stance that will end in futility, she decides to be "as cunning as a serpent but as harmless as a dove." With that she succeeds in enforcing her wish by getting her parents-in-law to acquiesce to her joining her husband in London. Akunna in *The Bride Price* does not abandon her-self to be forcefully married off to a deformed complex-ridden Okoboshi; but positivistically she contrives a way of escape though of a temporary nature, but that short twenty-four hour respite is all she needs at the time. Chike, the man of her heart is to effect their elopement a few hours later. Similarly, Ogbanje Ojebeta in *The Slave Girl* secures her release from the service of the Palagada household even against the odds and threats of the Palagada daughter, Miss Victoria who wants to inherit her. She puts up a fight and wins at the opportune time. Adah, in *Second Class Citizen,* forces her way into the classroom, that brazenness is to procure her an education and paves the way for better opportunities.

Basically, that is the thematic message of Buchi Emecheta, that the female, even in face of an oppressive system of deep-rooted norms and practices and belief in female subordination, must strive and assert herself. Generally the author makes them succeed in this quest for self-assertion. In a way, passivity is acquiescence to the *status quo* and so a perpetuation of it. But an aggrieved female need shed no tears but must work out a strategy for survival and recognition.

The true test of the woman continues to be the marriage institution. In this closed-in arena every married woman is to fight out her survival as an individual. The marriage paradox lies in the fact that it is both sublimating and subsuming. Through it a woman attains a status acclaimed by society and fulfils her biological need of procreation and companionship. Through it too, the woman's place of second-rate is emphasised and too easily she is lost in anonymity to the benefit and enhancement of the household. Adah in *Second Class Citizen* is made to understand just that, she is married, and so is subsumed completely to her husband's people — her earnings, her attention, her entire self. This is heightened in her own case because she is estranged from her family for the non-payment of her bride price.

But by far the greatest test for a married woman is bearing children. Her entire life and happiness depends on this. This is the case of Nnu-ego in *Joys of Motherhood;* Unable to bear children in her union with Amatokwu, she is cast out of her husband's affections, moved to a nearby hut reserved for older wives and put to work in the farm — for "if you can't produce sons, at least you can help harvest yams."[8]

Fecundity is rife with its own risks. Adaku, mother of two daughters, is told in very certain terms: "Our life starts from immortality and ends in immortality. If Nnaife had been married to only you, you would have ended his life on this round of his visiting earth. I know you have children, but they are girls, who in a few years time will go and help build another man's immortality."[9] To Adaku therefore, "The message was clear: she was only a lodger, her position in Nnaife Owulum's household had not been ratified."[10] She has to carve a life of her own and seek fulfilment and realisation elsewhere, where success for the woman is not measured by the number of male children she has. She becomes a prostitute.

In outlining the joys of motherhood, Nnolim notes that "irony skirts those 'joys' as Emecheta clothes them with ambivalence."[11] The joys of motherhood can only be fully realized if after having children and caring for them and equipping them for life, they in reciprocate as is expected by taking care of their parents and brothers and sisters. Parents therefore expect to be pensioned by their children. Nnu-ego's children, the sons who are trained at school do not, and leave their parents still saddled with the training of the other children. The joys become sour as each child strives to go to college, to break away from the slum and depravity of their parents' environment. Oshia goes to the United States to be more educated, Adim persists through secondary school at St. Gregory's College and later goes to Canada. Taiwo marries well to an Ibuzo educated man in church, but Kehinde her twin sister the "deep one" runs away to a Yoruba man, the son of a butcher to get married. Only Taiwo of the grown children is a consolation to her parents.

Nnu-ego philosophizes on her situation, she who has been trained in the traditional ways of her people on the belief that children make a woman. "She had had children, nine in all — how was she to know that by the time her children grew up the values of her country, her people and her tribe would have changed so drastically, to the extent where a woman with many children could face a lonely old age, and maybe a miserable death all alone, just like a barren woman? She was not even certain that worries over her children would not send her to her grave before her *chi* was ready for her."[12]

What is her reward for motherhood? The flattery of dreamers like the lorry driver "Oh you are a rich madam. . . a son in America? Goodness, you must be full of joy, madam!" or a resounding funeral when she is past its joys? The question still remains, what really are the joys of motherhood on which so much premium is placed? Nnu-ego rationalizes that her own reward is not measurable in material artefacts as cars, clothes and jewellery, but rather is predicated on the satisfaction of bearing them, of being the instrument of their being and education and so of their success. "Her joy was to know that she had brought up her children when they had started out with nothing, and that those same children might rub shoulders one day with the great men of Nigeria. That was the reward she expected."[13] All in all, the only rose among these thorns is bearing them. "Sometimes seeing my colleagues, I wish I didn't have so many children. Now I doubt if it has all been worth it. It was true what they said she thought, 'that if you don't have children the longing for them will kill you, and if you do, the worring over them will kill you.'"[14]

It is important in reading Buchi Emecheta's novels to see the developmental nature of her exploration of the theme of female assertiveness in the various societal facets which enslave the female. *The Bride Price* and *Slave Girl* all depict the young adolescent female asserting herself. *Second Class Citizen* and *Joys of Motherhood* both depict women in the marriage institution, the actual test of feminism.

Second Class Citizen places Adah and Francis, both educated, in a modern setting, first the capital city of Lagos and later in the far-away London metropolis with its sophisticated bigotry against the black man. In this foreign arena, Adah breaks out on her own. *Joys of Motherhood* posits woman in the same marriage and motherhood situation but in semi-rural setting in the slums of Lagos. The environment heightens the tension and is decisive in the actions of the characters. In each situation the test is, how does a woman escape the tyranny of a tradition and a system, assert her individuality while still playing out the roles of daughter, wife, mother? In *Double Yoke,* Emecheta reaches the epitome of feminism. Here, Nko breaks all the rules and social norms which tradition places on the female: (1) you must be chaste and Nko fails on that score; (2) you must be faithful to your betrothed, and Nko fails there in her affair with Elder Professor Ikot; and (3) you must not bear children outside marriage. Nko expects a baby for the Professor and decides to have it. Emecheta shows that though Nko may fail on all three counts she succeeds as an individual who knows what she wants and set about it the way she knows how. She wants to succeed in life as a woman desirable in her own right and as a qualified educated woman, financially capable of looking after her aspirations. What actually does she have left after she has successfully violated all these social norms and respectability? Is she still a woman? Can she ever be married by any man? The true reason for marriage emerges — love and companionship. The sudden death of her father and Nko's helpless despair almost resulting in attempted suicide bring the boy and girl toward a full realisation of their love and need for each other. Here are two people in love but who are kept apart by social prejudices implanted in them since birth. All the dos and donts in male and female behaviour prove superficial and unable to stand the test and rigours of modern society. In the final analysis therefore, it is the *individual* who counts, the individual must satisfy himself and herself first, and then the society.

Emecheta presents a number of superstitions and beliefs of the African society and she develops her themes along these lines. Running through the rubric of *The Bride Price* and *Slave Girl* is the belief that if a man succeeded in cutting off a lock of a girl's hair she belonged to him for life. It was the surest way of forcing marriage on an unwilling girl. Ojebeta's patronizing aunt, Uteh, thus warns her against her preference for the new ways and modern marriage — "Just be very careful about this new Religion, otherwise an old farmer will cut a lock of your hair and you will have to marry him."[15] This thought haunts Akunna in *The Bride Price* and in defiance she shaves off her long locks to forestall any such move by her many suitors.

The morbid superstition that a girl who "wished to live long and see her children's children, she must accept the husband chosen for her by her people, and the bride price must be paid. If the bride price was not paid, she would never survive the birth of her first child,'[16] forms the core of the tragedy of Akunna. Having overcome the caste system and settled to a marriage of love, she is brought down by this vicious monster. Herein lies one of Buchi Emecheta's thematic irony. Akunna wins the battle but loses the war. Her death negates her entire struggle for freedom and she dies under the same yoke she seeks to overcome. This is a tragic ironic twist to a love story. Akunna suffers for her feminism.

Ojebeta is almost sacrificed on the altar of superstition over the non-repayment of her slave purchase money of eight pounds to Clifford, the surviving son of her owner, Ma Palagada. Only doom awaits unredeemed slaves. When the money is paid by Jacob, her husband, Ojebeta becomes a new kind of slave changing her master to her husband. This, in effect, reinforces the position of the woman where she is only too happy to be owned. The gradual change in this male ownership of the female whom he is married to is reflected in the court scene when Nnu-ego asserts that Nnaife her husband "owns her". Adaku is to educate her outside the court, "I'm afraid even that has changed. Nnaife does not own anybody, not in Nigeria today. But senior wife, don't worry. You believe in the tradition."[17]

The belief in reincarnation is the driving force and chief motivator of action of *Joys of Motherhood*. Nnu-ego is the reincarnated spirit of the beautiful slave girl who was reluctantly buried with her mistress. She had promised Agbadi, Nnu-ego's father, that she would reincarnate in his household not as slave but as a daughter, and when Nnu-ego was born, she carried a lump on her head, a reminder of her past life when she was clubbed into the grave. Her incipient infertility is blamed on the slave woman and later (so) is the death of her first son. With sacrifices, the slave woman allows her "dirty" children or children that will come to no good. And Nnu-ego too after her death refuses to grant requests of fertility to women who invoke her aid, completing the cycle of the implacably aggrieved female.

In her latest novel, *The Rape of Shavi* (1983), Buchi Emecheta moves from the individualistic to the communalistic. Both men and women are portrayed in their collective role within a system. The book is based in the prehistoric era of a black country. At first, the analogy seems obviously a silly one — the British counterpart of the shavi rides in an airplane and yet the Shavians never set eyes on the whiteman before and the comments and consternation are so outmoded that they are revolting. The plausibility of the tale that an

aircraft carrying seven people on board leaving the airfield at Colling-
dale in the heart of England crashed at a village that knew no other
people than their neighbours is stretched. The setting is that of a
fairy-tale, a mixture of Ibusa-Benin territory with a dash of Asaba
and a stretch of Sahara desert for full measure. The names are pot-
pourri: Shavi, Pavton, Kofi, Shoshovi, Mensa, Egbongele. Credibility
is entirely eroded with the irritating banality of a fairy tale setting,
transposed to a novel in 1966! Whatever happened to Emecheta here?

This fantasy can only be explained in a positivistic framework
as a means of a comparative analysis of two cultures, Nigerian and
British. And somehow, it is inconceivable that the British society
which can produce a private aircraft fitted with ultra-modern sophisticated equipment and flown by one who had been "one of the archi-
tects who perfected the nuclear bomb", should land in an African
village which had never seen an airplane and never seen a whiteman.
This is the main flaw of the story and setting — primitive man in the
twentieth century? This anomaly undercuts the effectiveness of the
comparison. The Shavians have not acquired the art of artificial kindness as the British; their kindness is humane and genuine. She adapts
the concept of the noble savage, and the Shavian way of kindness
without strings surprises Flip and his companions. Emecheta's point
really is that civilised nations have much to learn from the so-called
backward peoples.

Characters

There is a strong delineation between male and female characters and
this permeates both children and adults. In most of her novels, female
characters are the protagonists and actions revolve round them. They
are therefore given strong character traits to carry the story through.
The woman is presented in her accepted social roles as daughter, sister,
wife, mother, aunt and mistress. The distinctive point in Emecheta's
female characterisation is its uniqueness. The women excel in their
roles, they are forceful and articulate, thinking beings whom the
reader is brought to recognize and appreciate as individuals not types.
Each character brings to bear on a stifling situation her own peculiar
way of solving the problem, hence we appreciate them for what they
are and have become not so much what they are supposed to be.

The men, because of their limited education, secure only menial
jobs as washermen, cooks, stewards, labourers and grass-cutters. The
full effect of such jobs is to rid the men of their manhood, their inner strength and assertiveness. Cordelia, the wife of Ubani the cook,
confides in the worried Nnu-ego, "Men here are too busy being
whitemen's servants to be men. Their manhood has been taken away

from them. The shame of it is that they don't know it."[18] The effect
of their effeminacy and lack of effective control of the home is that
the women mind the homes and look after themselves, providing for
their needs and those of their children. It does appear that the female
character is brought into focus by placing her in the reversed role of
provider. She thereby gains added strength of character. The male
characters are appreciated in ways other than in their socio-cultural
role of provider. Thus Nnu-ego spites her husband for his menial job,
but respects and even brings herself to love him for his ability to
make her a mother. Similarly, Adah resents Francis' inability to pro-
vide for them but appreciates the fact that he is the father of her
children.

Much criticism has been levelled at Emecheta on her presentation
of male characters. I shall mention three of such criticism here.
Oladele Taiwo asserts:

> The novelist has done what she knows best how to do. She has created
> a world of women where for the most part, attempt to portray male
> characters in unfavourable light may be an intentional device to take it
> back on men because of the image of women in the novels written by
> men. For example, most male characters in *In the Ditch* are social
> misfits. Pa Palagada in *The Slave Girl* is a terror to the slaves. Nnaife in
> *Joys of Motherhood* and Francis in *Second Class Citizen* are irrespon-
> sible heads of families who are mostly insensitive to the needs of their
> wives and children. Chike in *The Bride Price* is probably the only
> acceptable important male character in these novels. But he is tainted
> with slave ancestry, which places some doubt on the validity of his
> actions.[19]

Catherine Acholonu feels that Emecheta "overstepped her
bounds" in her portrayal of male characters "in exaggerated state of
idiocy, irresponsibility and insensitivity (which) reduces the plausibility and reliability of her point of view."[20] Acholonu takes consolation that these descriptions are localized to Emecheta's native home
town, Ibusa and the Bendel Igbo, and is worried that foreign readers
of Emecheta may extend her assertions to generalised traits of women
in Africa. Of course they are more true than not.

Eustace Palmer writes, still on male characterisation, "It is possible to argue that there are elements of distortion and exaggeration in
Emecheta's works especially in her presentation of males, most of
whom turn out to be little better than monsters." And he explains
this by stating that Emecheta "maybe needs to exaggerate their brutality and unattractiveness to make her feminist points."[21] In another
article Palmer comments on the remanticisation of Chike and the
villainy of Okonkwo.[22]

Buchi Emecheta's male characterization is neither exaggerated nor contrived for the purpose of demeaning the male. The truth of the matter is that this is a realistic portrayal of men and events. The quaintness of this is that the truth had never been told before; that writers have not been so bold as to dip their hands in their autobiography and spread out all the hidden linen to public view. Buchi looked and portrayed life as she saw it, as she lived it and as she saw others live it at the place and time. It is no exaggeration, it is the truth.

Let us consider two male characters, Nnaife and Francis in *Joys of Motherhood* and *Second Class Citizen*. Nnaife's characterisation is realistic and true to life. He is a washerman, hardly a job for slim sophisticated males, and his employer Dr Meers calls him "baboon". Nnaife is short, stocky with a belly like a pregnant cow, pale skin, puffy cheeks and weak jaw. He is indeed a jelly of a man. It is the sign of the times and culture that such a man would be married for, and his marriage consummated the very day he sets eyes on his wife. Nnu-ego may be beautiful but she is a second-hand and feared barren and can only fall to the likes of Nnaife. The characterisation is apt through and through. If things were normal for beautiful well-born Nnu-ego, she would never have been given over to a wobbly-belly man, washer of women's underwear.

Francis' characterisation in *Second Class Citizen* is typical of the modern young man who wants marital status and benefits without responsibility. First, he does not pay the bride price and completely alienates Adah's family. Second, he has aspirations for higher education and is content to do what most of his young friends do: allow their wives to slave for them and see them through school. Francis' weakness of character is shown from the outset: his close dependence on his family, so that when he is removed from them he now hardly copes. Francis' kind pervade the British landscape, men who live off women and who try to assert their masculinity into the bargain. Francis is young, slim and comely unlike the stocky Nnaife, but he also has a weak character and when faced with problems in his home he resorts to violence and brute force.

Buchi Emecheta is realistic in her character portrayal, and her "sin" is that she has exposed what hitherto were bedchamber secrets, covered and sacrosanct for the sake of mere existence. By saying it as it is, she is forcing an awareness through exposure and we hope she succeeds in fostering an atmosphere of change in attitudes and beliefs.

Narrative and Linguistic Style

Buchi Emecheta is an artist of description; she uses language beautifully; she uses ornate and poetic lanaguage and which is also lucid and flows. Scenes and incidents as described in her novels come up readily alive in the mind of the reader. She excels in the description of characters and physiognomically makes the characters' physique reflect their actions. Two examples suffice here — the description of Pa Noble's race in *Second Class Citizen* and Ona the proud one in *Joys of Motherhood.*

> The noise subsided slowly, giving way to a smile on a face; the face of an old man. A face that had been battered by gallons of African rain burned almost to scorching point by years and years of direct Nigerian sun; and later on ravaged by many biting wintry winds in England; a face that was criss-crossed like a jute mat by bottled-up sorrows, disappointments and maybe occasional joys. It was all there, on Pa Noble's face, just like an indelible legend written by mother nature on one of her sons. He had a hollow in the middle of his neck. Two prominent bones formed a triangle which encased this hollow, and whenever Pa Noble talked, something that looked like a chunk of meat inside his gullet would dance frighteningly in this encased hollow and the onlooker would feel like asking him to stop talking. He reminded them of a dying old man eager to tell it all to the living world before he passed to the other side and his voice was silenced for ever. To press home his point, which he did very often, Pa Noble would gulp. (p.97)

No important details escape the skilled rendition of Emecheta. Her descriptions are not wasted but used toward the projection of the character's actions. Thus the wrinkled spent Pa Noble is the husband of the "large-boned Birmingham woman, still young and still pretty" and it becomes obvious that Mrs Noble is in charge there.

Ona, the paramour and wife of Agbadi is the mother of the main character Nnu-ego. Her love story forms the background to the unarrogant character and defiant nature. Emecheta captures these in a description of her.

> She was medium height, and had skin like that of half-tribe palm nuts, smooth light coffee in colour. Her hair closely cropped, fitted her skull like a hat atop a head that seemed to be thrust out of her shoulders by a strong, long powerful neck. When she walked, her expensive waistheads, made of the best coral, murmured, and for men raised in that culture, who knew the sound of each bead, this added to her allurement. She had been used all her life to walking in bush paths, so she knew the tricks of avoiding thorns, using the balls of her feet rather than putting her full weight on her soles. This gave her movement the air of a mysterious and yet exciting cat. She had a trick of pointing her chin forward, as if she saw with it instead of her eyes which were black-rimmed and seemed sunken into her head. . . . . . .Greenish-black tattoos stood out richly against her brown skin. Though she was always scantily dressed, she frequently made people aware of being a conservative, haughty presence, cold as steel and remote as any woman royally born. When she

sat, and curled her long legs together in feminine modesty, one knew
that she had style, this only daughter of Obi Umunna.[23]

Emecheta's foreign images give away her long sojourn in Britain.
She uses mostly African imagery but sometimes she slips into western allusions.[24] Women from fattening rooms are described as
"lumping and lolling like overfed seals."[25] This is a hard sight in the
Nigerian fauna, so is the image of a gliding eel (p. 15). Few African
writers would describe a winding road "like an orange ribbon running
in between groves of thick forest."[26] Adah in her temper gesticulates
wildly during her argument with Francis, "like the arms of a windmill
that had gone mad."[27] A rather familiar African image is that of
Professor Okot's jacket flapping up and down like "angry elephant
ears."[28] In *Second Class Citizen,* Emecheta achieves a hybrid Afro-
European analogy in her description of the old British landlady —
"They knocked at the door. A woman's small head popped out of a
window, like that of a tortoise sunning itself. The head was like a
mop being shaken at them." (p. 83)

The author's third person narrative presents an omniscient point
of view. The reader is taken through the characters' thought processes,
motives for action or reaction and the effects on others. But Emecheta's notable achievement is a deep psychological insight into
women's behaviour, the young adolescent girls' aspirations, women's
impression of the other sex and what they do at their spare time. The
emotional sharing of joys and sorrows at the sympathy between Nnu-
ego and Adaku after that fateful judgement on their disagreement;
and later after the court sentences Nnaife to prison. Both women feel
for and identify with each other the only way women could. And it
takes a woman to capture that

Positivism and Acculturation

Positivism is defined as a philosophical system of logical empiricism
attributed to Auguste Comte in the mid-nineteenth century France.
It recognises absolute positive facts based on logic and observable
phenomena only. Its scientific methodology rejects the intrusion of
the personal, of emotions, sense perceptions and metaphysics. Positivism is here used as a direct, forthright, positive approach in the delineation and solution of problems encountered by women in a pre-
judiced society. However, Howard A. Slaatte outlines the criticism
against positivistic philosophy as "the loss of human subject, the loss
of moral values, and the loss of social reference."[29] He asserts that
"positivism fosters a moral indifference and callousness that can be
most debilitating to our culture,"[30] western culture that is, but this
can also be applied to African culture.

The bane of feminism in Africa is its equation with acculturation, its rejection of one's own way of life tested and traditionally sanctioned over time. Women, marry the husbands chosen for you, serve your husbands, be submissive to them. Akunna, by rejecting the husband, forced on her, and eloping with the one of her choice, and Adah by procuring birth control gadgets without her husband's permission and finally packing out of her marital home, are being ethically and culturally nihilistic. For a woman in fighting for and procuring her right is of effect and essence fighting against the goal of culture and is branded iconoclastic,[31] accultural, one who breaks the cultural *status quo* and reverses the aims of tradition.

This too is the core of Petersen's argument in the theme of feminist approach in African literature with reference to *Song of Lawino* — "in refusing to admire Lawino's romanticized version of her obviously sexist society one tears away the carpet from under the feet of the fighter against cultural imperialism. Lawino has become a holy cow and slaughtering her and her various sisters is inevitably a betrayal, because they are inextricably bound up with the fight for African self-confidence in the face of Western cultural imperialism."[32] The fact is that both exist conjointly, women emancipation and cultural imperialism. If a woman keeps her place without asking questions then she is being cultural and non-western. If she asserts herself, i.e. if she is feministic, then she is deviant, un-African, and accultural. This then is the bane of feminism in Africa.

Ebeogu's criticism of iconoclasm in Emecheta's presentation of Igbo culture and world view hangs on this prong of cultural nihilism. Her mission which she maintains is iconoclastic, the "debunking of the myth of masculinity in the Igbo culture"[33] and showing through propaganda "the male chauvinistic perversions in an African culture." Ebeogu's grip is much on what she does as on how she does it. Emecheta, he asserts, lacked aesthetic distance which separates fiction from fact, novel from autobiography, "rather her prejudices and attitudes keep on asserting themselves."

Ebeogu's criticism smacks of that stifling-male chauvinism which Emecheta exposes in novels, but more importantly though, it points dangerously to cultural annihilation. Culture is dynamic and, like every human phenomenon, is subject to the pruning machinery of time which slices off outmoded parts to prune it to a modern, progressive, and more acceptable mould. Such a change is not only desirable but inevitable. It is one that societies and cultures cannot fight against. Time changes everything and must therefore mould anew the African attitude to women. Emecheta calls attention to this attitude by narrating many stories and incidents in the past and present generations and the goal of this is change. Taiwo affirms this when he writes that "these novels emphasize the need for change . . . . the novelist presents these changes as inevitable."[34] There is need therefore for a reconsideration of Ebeogu's position. The point is not whether change will come or whether it should be allowed but rather how to adapt to change as an integral part of an African living culture, not an oppressive static past. Like the killing of twins or forceful betrothal or female circumcision or high pride price, these negative aspects of our culture must be swept away and this is not iconoclastic or nihilistic but progressive.

One of Slaatte's criticisms of positivistic philosophy is the "loss of moral value". Nko's sexual escapades with the scheming Professor are condemnable both in the traditional and modern canon even with the latter's permissiveness. Nko's action is a betrayal which she herself knows too well. A woman need not degenerate to sexual acts as a means to an end. Mrs. Nwaizu articulates that clearly: "Get a good degree by working hard for it. It is easier to get a good degree using one's brain power than bottom power. They may try to tell you that your bottom power is easier and surer, don't believe them . . . Nko, you don't have to lower yourself to that level."[35] The point is that feminism need not degenerate to immorality and sexual promiscuity as a means open to women to attain their life's desires. And mature Mrs Nwaizu concludes "If you become promiscuous, which you are not, our men made you so." Should a woman allow herself to be made so it would be defeatist of the women's cause, the choice should always remain hers as it is Adaku's in *Joys of Motherhood*.

Emecheta succeeds in enriching African literature with the other
Emecheta succeeds in enriching African literature with the other point of view; that women are not the cheerful, contented females they are made out to be. They appear to be so because they had no voice, no way out. Now Emecheta's is the powerful female voice that is heard and resounds everywhere, at home and abroad.

REFERENCES

1. Chinua Achebe, *Arrow of God*, (Heinemann, 1964) p. 94. Eustace Palmer notes this complacency in the traditional woman as portrayed in earlier African novels in his article — "The Feminine Point of View: Buchi Emecheta's *Joys of Motherhood*", *African Literature Today* (ed.) Eldred D. Jones (Heinemann 1983) p. 38.

2. See Cyprian Ekwensi, *Jagua Nana.*
3. The novels selected for this analysis are *Second Class Citizen* (1974), *The Bride Price*, (1976), *The Slave Girl* (1977), *Joys of Motherhood* (1979), *Double Yoke* (1982), *The Rape of Shavi* (1983).
4. *Second Class Citizen*, p. 7.
5. *The Bride Price*, p. 9.
6. Ibid, p. 10. Afam Ebeogu accused Emecheta of misinterpreting the name Akunna to suit her motive. He contends that Akunna *inter alia* means one born into the bounty of the father. Not quite: it means wealth procured by the father. One who is the father's wealth deriving from the father. Emecheta's interpretation is stretched. See his article "Enter the Iconoclast: Buchi Emecheta and Igbo Culture", *Commonwealth* 7, 2, Spring, 1985.
7. *Second Class Citizen*, p. 30.
8. *Joys of Motherhood*, p. 33.
9. *Ibid.*, p. 166.
10. *Ibid.*, p. 167.
11. Charles E. Nnolim, "Mythology and the Unhappy Woman in Nigerian Fiction", Paper presented to the 6th International Conference of African Literature and the English Language, 6–10 May 1986 at the University of Calabar. p. 3.
12. *Joys of Motherhood*, p. 219.
13. *Ibid.*, p. 202.
15. *The Slave Girl*, p. 153.
16. *The Bride Price*, p. 168.
17. Umeh comments on this feature of the woman's failure to recognise personal oppression. See her paper – Dr Marie Umeh, "The Poetics of Thwarted Sensitivity", 6th International Conference on African Literature and English Studies, University of Calabar, 6–10 May, 1986, p. 6.
18. *Joys of Motherhood*, p. 218.
19. *Joys of Motherhood*, p. 51.
20. Catherine Acholonu, "Buchi Emecheta", The Guardian Literary Series, *The Guardian*, Saturday, January 25, 1986 p. 13.
21. Eustace Palmer, "Women Writers and the African Society", Tribune Review, *Nigerian Tribune*, Wednesday, March 19, 1986 p. 5.
22. See Eustace Palmer, "A Powerful female voice in the African Novel: Introducing the novels of Buchi Emecheta", *New Literature Review*. No. 11, ; , pp. 26–27.
23. *Joys of Motherhood*, p. 12.
24. See Palmer's comment on her use of unmodified standard English in "A Powerful Female Voice in the African Novel: Introducting the Novels of Buchi Emecheta", p. 28.
25. *The Double Yoke*, p. 103.
26. *Ibid.*, p. 139.
27. *Second Class Citizen*, p. 132.
28. *Double Yoke*, p. 83.
29. cf. Howard A. Slaatte, *The Dogma of Immaculate Perception: A Critique of Positivistic Thought*, Washington, University Press of America, 1979.
30. *Ibid.*, p. 99.
31. See Afam Ebeogu's vitriolic title "Enter the Iconolast: Buchi Emecheta and the Igbo Culture", *Commonwealth* Vol. 7, 2, Spring 1985.
32. Kirsten Holest Petersen, "First Things First: Problems of a Feminist Approach to African Literature"*Kunapipi* (ed.) A, na Rutherford, Aarhus, VI, 3, 1984, p. 39.

33. Ebeogu, p. 83.
34. Taiwo, pp. 112--113.
35. *Double Yoke*, p. 155.

BUCHI EMECHETA

Born in Lagos in 1944, to Ibusa parents. She had her primary school education at Ladilak School and Reagan Memorial Baptist School, both in Yaba, Lagos and went to Methodist Girls High School (MGHS) Yaba at the age of ten for her secondary education. Obtained an honours degree in Sociology from London University. She has worked as a Teacher, Librarian, and Community Worker. She has written articles for the *New Statesman* and for the *Time Educational Supplement,* Television and Radio Plays. Appointed Senior Research Fellow in 1980 at the university of Calabar, Department of English and Literary Studies, she is presently a member of the Advisory Council to the British Home Secretary of Race and Equality, and serves on the Arts Council of Great Britain. Currently living in North London, where she has been since 1962. A mother of five children.

Publications

The Ditch, London: Barrie and Jenkins, 1972
Second Class Citizen. New York: George Braziller, 1975
The Bride Price. New York: George Braziller, 1976
The Slave Girl. London: Allison and Busby, 1979
The Joys of Motherhood. London: Allison and Busby, 1979
The Moonlight Bride. Oxford University Press, (Masquerade Books,) 1980
The Wrestling March. Oxford University Press (Masquerade Books) 1980.
Destination Biafra. London: Allison and Busby, 1981
Naira Power: London: Macmillan, 1981
Double Yoke, London: *Ogwugu Afor,* 1981; and *The Rape of Shavi,* 1983

Works About Her

Ebeogu, Afam, 'Enter the Iconoclast: Buchi Emecheta and the Igbo

Culture', *Commonwealth, Essays and Studies.* Vol. 7, No. 2, 1985 pp. 83—93.

Kerridge, Roy; 'More White Mischief', *Times Literary Supplement* 3, Feb. 1984 p. 116. (Discusses Buchi Emecheta)

Lauer, Margaret Read; Buchi Emecheta: "The Bride Price" In *World Literature Written in English,* 16, No. 2 (November, 1977) p. 310.

Murray, Maggie and Emecheta, Buchi; Our Own Freedom (On Women in Africa). London: Sheba Feminist Publishers, 1981.

Palmer, Eustace; The Feminine point of view: Buchi Emecheta's *The Joys of Motherhood, African Literature Today 31: Recent Trends in the Novel,* Heinemann, London: 1983. p. 38—55.

Wilson, Judith; Buchi Emecheta: Africa From a Woman's View, in *Essence,* February, 1980 p. 12.

Umeh, Marie; African Women in Transition in the Novels of Buchi Emecheta, *Presence Africaine,* 116—4, 1980, pp. 190—201.

Collins, H; Emecheta, Buchi, The Bride Price reviewed, *World Literature Today.* L1(3) 491.

The Bride Price Reviewed, *West Africa* 3084 (1976) 1145

'A Worshipper from Afar', interview by Tunde Obadina, in *Punch* (Nigeria), 17 May 1979.

Chapter 2

The Works of Flora Nwapa

Dr Yemi I. Mojola

Flora Nwapa occupies the unique position of being the first Nigerian female novelist whose work was published. Her fictional production consists of four full-length novels: *Efuru* (1966), *Idu* (1971), *One is Enough* (1981), *Women are Different* (1986), and a much shorter one, *Never again* (1975). A versatile writer, her literary talent has also manifested itself, not only in the publication of collections of short stories, *This is Lagos and other Stories* (1971) and *Wives at War and other Stories* (1980), but also in the area of children's literature where she has published several stories for children of primary school age. Her recent publication of *Cassava Song & Rice Song* launches her into the world of poetry.

These works which are sociological in conception are set generally in well-defined dimensions of time and space. The setting of *Efuru* and *Idu* is a traditional society in the Oguta area of Igboland in the early colonial period although the colonial presence surfaces only rarely. *Never Again* is set in this same area, the native milieu of the author, but during the Nigerian Civil War of 1967 to 1970 and therefore in a contemporary period, whereas in the former works, the area is in Nigeria at a time of peace. A historical fact is thus reflected in the spatial organisation of the novels.

The two most recent novels move out of this local setting into cosmopolitan environment, thereby giving a more national outlook to Nwapa's literary inspiration. *One is Enough* unfolds partly in Onitsha and partly in Lagos during the post-independence civilian regime and that part of the military interregnum culminating in the *coup d'etat* of 1975. *Women are Different* opens in January 1945, although the narrator utilises the flashback technique to narrate an event which occurred in 1944 and which serves as the introduction to the novel. A specific data reference suggests that the novel ends in 1975. The setting of this novel is highly fragmented — several towns in the eastern part of Nigeria and in the defunct 'Biafra', Lagos, Benin, London, Hamburg and so on — thus creating an unnecessary diffusion in the spatial configuration of the novel.

All the novels of Nwapa except *Never Again,* the fictional version of the Nigerian Civil War from a 'Biafran' woman's viewpoint, have the same plot pattern: the narration of the life history of a central fictitious character or characters. *Never Again,* on the contrary, concentrates on a slice not only of the life of Kate, the narrator, but also of that of the whole community. With deep insight, the psychological and physical stresses of the war on the individual and the collectivity are vividly portrayed.

While there is correlation between the title and plot and the thematic focus in the first four novels, the same can hardly be said of the last one, *Women are Different.* The author, rather than show a mastery of the art of fiction through maturity in the creative domain, compounds some of the flaws in the former works and generates new ones. For example, the content of the novel hardly justifies its title. The plot degenerates into the melodramatic in parts such as when the boys of Okrika Grammar School walk home the girls of ACMGS, a walk of about eighteen to twenty kilometres, at night and return to their school the same night. Even if this event is a real life experience, it is not a singular event but an event of universal application which make accomplished fiction. In addition, a lot of material which does not contribute to the advancement of the plot such as the visit of Janet, the mad woman, to Rose are detrimental to the success of the narration.

Nwapa's fictional universe is a world of women for all her central characters and most of her secondary characters are women. Their daily activities within and outside the home, their cultural and religious observances and beliefs, their individual and collective interactions with one another and with men, especially in *Efuru* and *Idu,* constitute a solid structure documenting certain aspects of the traditional way of life of the Igbo people. On the contrary, the *raison d'etre* of the male characters resides in their being husbands or lovers to the female characters or in their being consulted as 'dibias' (medicine-men) by anguished infertile or barren women seeking their aid in order to have children. Women tower over men in mental and material achievements. Men are often regarded as nothing more than instruments for procreation as in *One is Enough,* where the protagonist, Amaka, who had to separate from her husband due to her infertility and its consequent problems, seduces Father Mclaid and eventually has twin sons for him but rejects his hand in marriage even though he has resigned from the priesthood in order to marry her. Whether as husbands or lovers, men are generally portrayed as irresponsible, immoral exploiters existing in the shadow of the women sometimes as mere nonentities like the two husbands of Efuru, the central character in *Efuru*.

Efuru and Idu, the protagonist in *Idu*, are the author's most attractive creations although Idu does not attain the immense stature of Efuru. They resemble each other in several moral and physical traits. Endowed with great beauty, intelligence and independent minds, they become wealthy through a remarkable business acumen and unparalleled industry. In the community, they are reputed for their benevolence, innate goodness and excellence as wives, for they are 'full of sense and understanding'. Both face an almost intractable problem: infertility. However, while Efuru's two marriages fail, Idu's marriage is very harmonious. We consider these near-perfect characters as Nwapa's vision of the ideal Igbo woman rather than as representing the ordinary Igbo woman. In their day to day activities however, they are just like other women.

In general, Nwapa's female creations are industrious, businesslike and economically independent, pursuing with seriousness of purpose and determination whatever they have set their minds upon. For example, Agnes, one of the main chracters in *Women are Different* would have remained semi-literate but for her resolution to acquire a sound education. Having escaped being married off to a much older man of dubious character while still in the secondary grammar school, through hard work and good behaviour she is forced into marriage with the same man immediately after her final examination. But after having four children, in spite of her husband's opposition, she struggles on to earn a University degree and ends up with a well-paying job.

Despite the common characteristics identified above, the female characters are not homogeneous in their attitude to life. Three main categories are discernible. Constituting one group are the purely traditional illiterate women like Efuru, Idu, Ajanupu (Efuru's aunt-in-law), Amaka's mother and Amaka's mother-in-law. Traditional culture and religion inform the attitude of these women who abhor all forms of deviant behaviour such as adultery and prostitution.

The intermediate category consists of educated women who were adolescents in the forties and fifties like the protagonists of *Women are Different*, Agnes, Dora and Rose, whose European names are a direct result of the impact of Western education and religion on the society. Influenced by the christian moral values passed on to them by their missionary teachers rather than their native Igbo culture, they frown on the corruption, immorality and extreme materialism of the seventies, but they engage in legally unsanctioned sexual relationships. The portrayal of this side of their life underscores a social phenomenon: the biological need for sexual satisfaction of relatively young women who are separated or divorced from their husbands, or those like Rose who are professionally recognised and materially comfortable, but who are single.

The third group is composed of women devoid of moral values such as the members of the Cash Madam Club in *One is Enough,* Comfort, a classmate of Dora, Agnes and Rose, who as far back as her first year in the secondary school in 1945, has been corrupt and Chinwe and Zizi, daughters of Dora and Agnes respectively. These woman epitomise some of the ills of a corrupt society, the Nigerian society: avarice, selfishness, corruption and self-degradation for financial gratification.

The dominant thematic interest in all the novels except *Never Again* is the woman. Based on her knoweldge of the way of life of the Igbos in particular and of Nigerians in general, Nwapa exposes the woman's situation within traditional and contemporary societies, especially her role as wife and mother. She focuses on the importance attached to having children and thereby stresses the unenviable lot of infertile or barren women within the community. She examines the necessity for economic independence through determination and hard work, a *sine qua non* for self-fulfilment and freedom of action for a woman. Another theme recurring in most of the works is the inexorable control of fate over man's existence. In *Never Again,* the tragedy of war is portrayed while in *One is Enough* and especially *Women are Different,* various ills plaguing the Nigerian society since independence are highlighted.

In *Efuru, Idu* and *One is Enough,* Nwapa doggedly examines the question of childlessness in marriage with its attendant problems. Igbo traditional society views with utter dismay and ridicule a marriage without issue, an attitude repeatedly reflected in the novels. "It was a curse not to have children.....
It was regarded as a failure." *(Efuru,* p. 165).
"What is important is not marriage as such,
but children..... A marriage is no marriage without
children" *(One is Enough,* p. 10)
In contemporary Nigeria, a childless marriage is still generally considered a mishap.
"A childless marriage cannot last in the Nigeria of today." *(One is Enough,* p. 37)
But it is the woman who invariably is blamed for the situation and she is subjected to all sorts of indignities.like being called a man especially in the traditional milieu. Efuru, Idu and Amaka experience intense anguish due to their infertility. Efuru's acclaimed excellence in all spheres of domestic life does not save her from being abandoned

by two husbands. Subsequently, she returns to her father's house. And like the beautiful and wealthy goddess Uhamiri, the Woman of the Lake, whose votary she is, she finds perfect peace in the dedication of her life to the service of humanity. Uhamiri has 'never experienced the joys of motherhood', yet she is happy and women worship her goodness. This is the message of *Efuru:* motherhood is not the only path to happiness and contentment. A woman can lead a life of fulfilment through selfless service to others.

Idu's case presents another picture. After several years of marriage, she has a baby boy but four years elapse before she becomes pregnant again. In the course of her pregnancy, her beloved husband, Adiewere, suddenly passes away. Idu consequently loses the will to live and passes away, the budding life developing in her notwithstanding. This unexpected denouement has been criticised as being too far-fetched and therefore an artistic flaw. But Ernest Emenyonu argues that it is remote only to those who do not "understand that even among the Igbo, the love between two individuals can be such that one can die without the other." In spite of this explanation, the stress on the indispensability of children which pervades the novel would generate doubts about the logic of Idu's death bearing in mind her pregnancy, the fact that she already has a son and her strength of character. The message of *Idu* can thus be summarised: a woman should do all she can to preserve a harmonious marriage built on love like the marriage of Adiewere and Idu.

In *One is Enough,* published exactly ten years after the publication of *Idu,* the novelist offers another option to women. Amaka's husband prefers an illiterate imbecile to his educated, loving, industrious and prosperous wife due to her infertility after six years of marriage. She makes a clean break from him but refuses to marry the man of whom she eventually has children, having realised that she does not need a second husband. She decides to devote herself to promoting her already flourishing contract business and bringing up her children. Amaka's decision demonstrates that a woman should not tolerate a bad husband. After the break up of a marriage, if a woman can have children for another man, she should do so without feeling obliged to marry him. But she must be economically independent.

The solutions identified so far, though laudable, have not struck at the root of the problem: the fact that the society must change its attitude towards the woman, marriage and motherhood, which, desirable as it is, constitutes only an option.

Although the infertility theme is of no interest in *Women are Different,* other problems faced by women are portrayed. It is in this novel that the narrator states unequivocally the proper perspective in which the society must view the woman:

> Chinwe had done the right thing. Her generation was doing better than·
> her mother's own. Her generation was telling the men, that there are
> different ways of living one's life fully and fruitfully. They are saying
> that women have options. Their lives cannot be ruined because of a bad
> marriage. They have a choice to marry and have children, a choice to
> marry or divorce their husbands. Marriage is not the only way. *Women
> Are Different*, p. 119

Chinwe has just divorced her husband without demanding mainten-ance allowance for the children. Unfortunately, Chinwe is a negative example of womanhood. Chinwe's generation is making its wealth by dubious means and therefore is not worthy to be the yardstick for determining the emancipation of women. A generation of sober, self-respecting, industrious and determined women would have been more appropriate. Certain other conceptual flaws occur in this novel. For example, Rose, a professionally competent spinster is portrayed as the loser among all the characters on account of her advanced age and her not having a husband, a lover nor children. Is spinsterhood not one of those choices open to women as "there are different ways of living one's life fully and fruitfully"?

The necessity for economic independence on women's part through industry and firmness of purpose constitutes one of Nwapa's favourite themes, for she firmly believes that it is the surest means by which a woman can reject all social shackles. In her fictional works, women participate in all aspects of the economic life of their com-munities as traders and farmers in the traditional and rural milieu and as teachers, administrators and business women in contemporary and urban milieu. Efuru and Idu stand out through the nature and volume of their trading activities which surpass those of men. The dedication of *One is Enough,*

> For Ine, my husband's mother who believes that all women married or
> single must be economically independent.

represents an eloquent testimony of the author's concern about women's economic independence.

Numerous references are made to God's omnipotence, omniac-tion and omniscience specially in *Idu* where "Everything is in the hands of God" becomes a leitmotiv. In *Efuru,* the power of the lesser deities, especially Uhamiri, and the 'chi' or personal god of each indi-vidual, is evoked whenever human understanding fails to comprehend a phenomenon. In *One is Enough* adverse incidents derive from fate.

The dependence on the controlling influence of the supernatural on man's life alleviates the traumatic effects of misfortunes on the female characters. This trust in a power or in powers which direct man's path through life points to the importance of religion among the Igbo. It is significant that in *Women are Different,* references to fate are absent.

In *One is Enough* and *Women are Different,* Flora Nwapa exposes some of the ills destroying the Nigerian body politic and traces some of them to the immaturity, irresponsibility and unpreparedness of the politicians who took over the reins of government from the British at independence. Social decadence manifested at personal and public levels reached alarming proportions in the wake of the civil war which gave rise to unprecedented unethical behaviour . However, certain conceptual contradictions are discernible. For example, the depiction of the female characters on whose actions the author formulates her thesis about women's freedom is at variance with some of her criticisms of the society. The contemporary women who are economically independent through business such as Amaka and Chinwe, though hard-working, make their initial and even subsequent financial gains through debauchery and corruption.

The author's experiences of the civil war gave her the opportunity to express her views on war in fictional form. In effect, *Never Again* is a denunciation of the Nigerian Civil War in particular, and of all wars and all forms of violence in general. Kate, on the 'Biafran' side, is the author's spokesman. Foremost among those who see through the false war propaganda, she experiences much mental agony in having convictions which are contrary to the general opinions nurtured by blind patriotism. Kate's moral courage and strength of character support her in this situation. War is shown to be a tragedy which accentuates man's frailties: collective and individual selfishness, deceit, brutality, corruption, cowardice and other forms of inhumanity. The physical and psychological ravages of war, the uncertainties, the trauma of sudden evacuation from familiar and loved surroundings, and above all, the fear of death are made a vivid reality.

All the works of Nwapa published after the Nigerian Civil War except the stories for children, contain references to aspects of the war. In her first collection of short stories, *This is Lagos and other Stories,* two stories reflect events concerning the war while the others depict vividly situations from everyday life in some big cities across the country — Kaduna, Onitsha, Benin, Port-Harcourt, Enugu and especially, Lagos, with its degenerate culture. The stories focus on all sorts of societal problems. Difficulties confronting women particularly in their relationship with men are viewed from various perspectives.

Difficulties such as the desire of men to exploit women sexually, male infidelity and incomprehension, the agony of childlessness leading a wife to depression and crime, the deceit and exploitation of widows by all including close relatives. Nwapa goes beyond these mainly feminine concerns and examines other fundamental issues such as the unpredictability of death and the anguish and bitter disappointment of parents whose promising children end up as failures through criminal association.

In the more recent collection of short stories, *Wives at War and other Stories,* women are involved in all kinds of war. For example, in "The Chief's Daughter", Adaeze fights against the obnoxious Igbo traditional practice whereby a beloved daughter becomes a 'legal' prostitute by having children for her father by any man. The first three stories are set in 'Biafra'. They show the tragic effect of war on children and the opposing attitudes of women on the 'Biafran side to the war; some are hawks while others are bent on returning to a life of security and peace with their families. In the other four, the writer analyses the complexities of human relationships at different levels such as sex and race. As usual all the stories are centred around women whose problems Nwapa probes with the insight of an insider.

Flora Nwapa's mastery of the art of story-telling is evident from her ability to vary her style to suit the nature of a work and the emotion of the moment. In *Efuru* and *Idu,* proverbs, imagery, Igbo sentence structures as well as direct Igbo expressions which cannot be translated or whose effect cannot be properly communicated by equivalents in the English language, are generously used to season conversations and descriptions. These stylistic aspects which confer a distinctive tone on *Efuru* and *Idu* are rare in the other works which are contemporary in setting.

On the other hand, in *Never Again,* the use of extremely short sentences creates a broken rhythm which corresponds to the broken pace of the lives of the characters in the war situation. At the most critical moments, the sentences are shortest, thus accentuating the tension:

> We stood. Others joined us. Watched. Then a rocket, another and yet another. We took cover. We lay on our stomachs. The body was peaceful. *(Never Again,* p. 56).

A pregnant woman has just died on the road while in labour. In the same novel and in some of the short stories, the use of rhetorical questions at moments of mental tumult, the grim humour and the stinging irony give tremendous force to the ideas expressed. The point of view in *Never Again* and in a few of the short stories is subjective; in effect the narrations are in the first person, implying that the narrators are personally involved in the events narrated. The point of view thus reinforces the impression already created by the setting and the subject matter that the works are based on reality. But in *Women are Different,* which is narrated in the third person, authorial interventions, through the use of first person pronouns, represent an inconsistency in the point of view.

Apart from the works in prose, Flora Nwapa has made her first attempt at composing poems with the publication of *Cassava Song & Rice Song.* "Cassava Song" is a glorification and personification of Cassava as Mother, "the giver of life", the patient nourisher of man in all circumstances. Since Cassava grows in any soil and since it is used as food in various forms by Nigerians, its cultivation should be given priority. But "Rice Song" is a strong condemnation of the importation of rice. The author urges the government to ban its importation which she sees as a contrivance of the powerful to amass more wealth. While the ideas in these "Songs" are valuable, the compositions, especially "Rice Song", lack the essential qualities of poetry such as economy of language and the use of symbolic expressions and imagery. "Cassava Song" possesses a few characteristics of poetry but "Rice Song" is absolutely prosaic.

In spite of the serious artistic and conceptual flaws noticeable in a few of her novels, Flora Nwapa has established herself as a novelist and short story-writer of note. Her works consistently reveal her commitment to the cause of women and her concern for their freedom from all practices and beliefs which impede their material and spiritual progress. In addition, her concern for the improvement of the Nigerian society is obvious in her criticism of societal ills. Her novels which are based on Igbo traditional life show the illusory nature of the claim of superiority of the Igbo man over the Igbo woman. Her works constitute a testimony of the indispensability of the woman in the social and economic life of Nigeria. But above all, the works demonstrate the confidence the author has in the ability of women to lead a life of fulfilment within or outside marriage unfettered by men, provided they are economically independent.

FLORA NWAPA

Flora Nwapa was born at Oguta in Imo State of Nigeria. Educated at C.M.S. Central School, Lagos 1936–1944; A.C.M.G.S. Elelenwa 1945–1948; C.M.S. Girls School, Lagos 1949–1950; University

College, Ibadan 1955–57 and obtained B.A. (London) degree. She also holds a diploma in Education from the University of Edinburgh 1957–1958. She is the first Nigerian woman novelist and publisher and has held numerous posts such as Woman Education Officer (Queen's School, Enugu) 1958–1962; Assistant Registrar (Public Relations) University of Lagos, Lagos 1962–1967; Commissioner and member of the Executive Council of East Central State of Nigeria: Ministries of Health and Social Welfare; Lands, Survey and Urban Development; and Establishments 1970–1975. A visiting lecturer in creative writing, Alvan Ikoku College of Education, Owerri 1976 – 1977. Her awards include Distinguished Alumni award, University of Ibadan, 1982; Officer of the Order of the Niger (OON) 1983; Certificate of participation – Iowa University School of Letters International Writing Programme 1984; Merit award for Authorship/ Publishing, University of Ife Book-fair 1985. Enjoys Swimming and dancing. Married to Gogo Nwakuche, an industrialist. They have three children. Flora Nwapa is presently a Writer and Publisher; Managing Director, Tana Press Limited and Flora Nwapa Books Limited both in Enugu. Her contact address is 2A Menkiti Lane, Ogui, Enugu, Anambra State, Nigeria.

Publications

Efuru, London: Heinemann, 1966
Idu. London: Heinemann, 1970, 282 p.
This is Lagos and other Stories. Enugu: Nwamife, 1971.
Emeka-driver's Guard. London: University of London Press, 1972.
Mummy Water. Enugu: Flora Nwapa Books, 1979.
The Miracle Kittens. Enugu: Flora Nwapa Books, 1980.
My Tana Colouring Book. Enugu: Flora Nwapa Books, 1979.
Adventures of Deke. Enugu: Flora Nwapa Books, 1980.
Journey to Space. Enugu: Flora Nwapa Books, 1980.
Wives at War and Other Stories. Enugu: Tana Press, 1980.
My Animal Number Book. Enugu: Flora Nwapa Books, 1981.
One is Enough. Enugu: Tana Press, 1982.
Never Again. Enugu: Tana Press, 1984.
Cassava Song and Rice Song. Enugu: Tana Press.
Women are Different. Enugu: Tana Press, 1986.

Other Publications

'Ada' Black Orpheus III4 (1976) 20–30; Chap. 1 of unpublished novel of that name.

'Idu' In *African Arts/Arts d'Afrique,* Vol I No. 4 Summer 1968, p. 50—2

'My Spoons are finished' In *Presence Africaine,* 67, No. 63, 0.227 — 35 (Short Story).

This is Lagos Interlink, 2(3) 1966, 10—2

Works About Her

1. Asanbe, Joseph: 'The Place of the Individual in the Novels of Chinua Achebe, T.M. Aluko, Flora Nwapa and Wole Soyinka', Indiana University, 1979. 205 pages. (40:5447A).
2. Conde, Maryse: "The Female Writers in Modern Africa: Flora
3. Nwapa. . . . . ." in *Presence Africaine,* No. 82, 1972, pp. 132—43. Emenyonu, Ernest N. "Who does Flora Nwapa write for?" *In African Literature Today:* a Review edited by Eldred Jones. No. 7: Focus on Criticism. London: Heinemann, 1975 p. 28—33.
4. Mojola, Yemi: "Flora Nwapa" in *The Guardian,* 23 November, 1985, p. 13.
5. Ogan, Amma: "Flora Nwapa: The Stories of Women Come Naturally to me" in *The Guardian,* 24 March 1985, pp. 4 and 10.
6. Ojo-Ade, Femi: "Female Writers, Male Critics". In *African Literature Today* 13; Recent Trends in the Novel, London: Heinemann, 1983, pp. 159—178. (Treats Buchi Emecheta and Flora Nwapa).
7. Taiwo, Oladele: "Flora Nwapa": in *Female Novelists of Modern Africa.* London: Macmillan, 1984. pp. 47—83.

Reviews

Efuru. Reviewed in *Ba Shiru,* Journal of the Department of African Languages and Literature, University of Wisconsin, Madison, Vol. 1 No. 2, Spring 1970, pp. 58—61. Reviewer: Emenyonu, Ernest N.

Efuru. Reviewed in *Educ. Herald* 1, a, 1966, 18—19, Reviewer. Caroline Ifeka.

Idu. Reviewed in *African Literature Today,* No. 5, 1971, pp. 150—153. Reviewer Adeola A. James.

Idu. Reviewed in *Nigeria Magazine,* 89, 1966. 131—132, 141. Reviewer: Caroline Ifeka.

Chapter 3

The Writings of Ifeoma Okoye
Charles Nnolim

After Cyprian Ekwensi, the field of literature for children and adolescents seems to have become dominated by our female writers. Flora Nwapa naturally led the way and when she established her own publishing house, TANA Press, the Press became dedicated to publishing children's literature as its area of primary concern.

Ifeoma Okoye joined the bandwagon of writers of children's literature on her discovery that there were few children's books on the Nigerian market written by Nigerian writers, "books with Nigerian background. . .and with Nigerian children as characters" (*The Guardian*, November 10, 1985 p.9). The sequel was a veritable literary harvest for children: *No School For Eze; No Supper for Eze; Only Bread for Eze;* all published by Fourth Dimension. Flora Nwapa's TANA Press published the popular *Eze Goes to School* and *The Adventures of Tulu,* while Macmillan published the longest of them all, *Village Boy* which is now a required reading in Anambra State Secondary Schools. Teresa Meniru *(Footsteps in the Dark; Unoma; Unoma at College; Dreams of Joy; The Bad Fairy and The Caterpillar; The Melting Girl and other Stories; The Carver and the Leopard),* and Charry Ada Onwu *(One Bad Turn; Ifeanyi and Obi)* are fellow women who are gaining equal attention as female writers of children's literature on the current literary scene.

Village Boy (1981, Macmillan) really needs a sequel. It tells the unfinished story of Joseph whose paternal uncle agrees, with great reluctance, to sponsor his secondary school career with the proviso that 'after the first term if he does not do well enough to satisfy me, I'll withdraw my help. I have no money to waste."

True to the pattern of such adolescent literature, Joseph, a village boy with real village ignorance and mannerisms, experience difficulties and disappointments. His English is so poor that one of the tutors, Mr. Uche, in despair tells Joseph before all other students in class: "You are not fit to be in this school. Sit down!" Moreover, Joseph is harassed by Chu-boy, a spoilt loud-mouthed brat from a rich family, because Joseph confesses honestly that he it was who held a midnight birthday party, contrary to the school regulations. Furthermore, Joseph's mother had an operation in the hospital and he had to leave school to attend to her. In the interim, he is accused of stealing a fellow student's money, a false accusation that is spearheaded by a spiteful Chu-boy and the threat of expulsion hangs over his head.

But life has its compensations. Joseph is strong in mathematics. Fellow classmates, Adamu and Jegede, love him and give him extra lessons in English. The lost money is discovered in a book borrowed from and returned by another boy, to the library. Joseph is transparently honest and is really hardworking. At the end of the school year he passes his examinations and is promoted. His uncle, Jude, has no choice but to keep him in school. The lesson for the young audience is straightforward: Honesty and hard-work are the only avenues to success. In this day and age, one wonders whether Ifeoma Okoye should not have added something which all young men lack or ignore: devout attitude to religion and fervent prayers!

II

With *Behind the Clouds* (Longman, Drumbeat Series, 1982), Ifeoma Okoye moves on to more serious literature addressed to young adults without excluding adolescents and children in the book's concerns. Where does one draw the line, one might ask, between adolescent literature and literature for mature minds? The answer will shortly emerge.

In the interim, let's focus attention on the landscape of Ifeoma Okoye's fictional world in *Behind the Clouds*. The contours of that landscape trace a story-line conceived in irony and ended in irony, leading to the circular structure of the novel.

Ije, the good-natured wife of the loving and hard-working, successful architect, Dozie, is presumed barren, and a great deal of anxiety and money are expended on her "cure", while it is Dozie who is sterile all along. At last, after Dozie "proves" his manhood by supposedly making the sassy, rude Virginia of easy virtue pregnant, it dawns on Dozie through Virginia's tactless taunts that Dozie cannot impregnate any woman. Dozie consequently goes for a test overseas and regretfully admits to Ije:

> I'm sorry that you've submitted yourself to all kinds of treatment, unpleasant ones and dangerous ones', when I have all along been the cause of our childlessness.

So, the book begins to end where it should all have started. Dozie goes to seek a cure he should have sought from the beginning. Ije is now let off the hook which Dr. Melie should have done from the beginning. Ije *returns* to her house from which she had packed out because of the Virginia imbroglio. Virginia returns to nowhere since she comes from nowhere. Dozie, it is imagined, will take complete control of his family affairs which he had allowed his kith and kin to interfere with. Behind every cloud, there is always a silver lining! In sum, *Behind the Clouds* is a moral fable. Ifeoma Okoye arrives first at a moral conclusion: It is not right to blame all cases of infertility and childlessness on the wife, and drown her in drugs and subject her to all kinds of psychological tortures, without also testing the man to ascertain his potency. Ancillary to this is her protest against the part played by ignorant kith and kin, especially mother-in-law anxious for grand children, in ruining the happiness of an otherwise loving couple by suggesting a second wife for the man who, in Ije's and Dozie's case actually is to blame. The same reason pushes Beatrice to allow the false prophet and faith healer, Apostle Joseph, to make her pregnant so that she could feel secure in her marital home.

In pursuit of her thesis, the author's voice becomes rather too insistent as she indicts meddlesome relatives of the childless couple who continue to exempt the man from all blame or even suspicion of blame by acting as a wedge between him and his wife, even when the man, like Dozie, initially does not seem to mind. In the same voice, the author indicts in unmistakable terms prayer-houses that exploit anxious women desperately looking for children by exposing them to temptation and in the process, milking them of large sums of money. While Beatrice succumbs and confesses to Ije that she was carrying Apostle Joseph's child in order to have some peace of mind and a hold on her husband and a secure place in her family, Ije successfully resists. Furthermore, that the "famous" Dr. Melie fails to ask Ije to bring along her husband for tests after she found nothing wrong with Ije but proceeds to "treat" her in spite of all the indicators of healthy organs in her, further indicts the so-called enlightened medical practitioners who, because they are culture-bound, neglect to treat the man as well. The novel becomes an all-round indictment of society's attitude to childless women in our culture; for it is this attitude that pushes childless women to desperate "cures", just to have children. This leads Ifeoma Okoye to her central thesis: *it takes two to have a childless marriage. The man should also submit himself to a cure.*

Attention was drawn earlier to what makes *Behind the Clouds* adolescent rather than adult literature. It is the lack of depth, the lack of subtlety, the too-insistent voice on what constitutes the moral or the theme without making large allowances for the imagination to gather in the debris of unexplained meanings and implications. There are no mystifications, and no fuzzying of the edges to admit of secondary interpretations. All the characters of Ifeoma Okoye are secondary interpretations. All the characters of Ifeoma Okoye are types. Ife is too good a wife to even exchange a harsh word with the wicked mother-in-law. Where she is insulted, she returns love. To neither her mother-in-law who obviously sees no good in her nor to Virginia who intrudes into her family with obvious crudity and extreme bad manners, does she ever give a piece of her mind. In addition, she is shown to be nothing less than a saint in skirts. She surrenders all her salary to her husband whom she educated by holding down two jobs in England, and when he asks for forgiveness in the end, she readily accepts him back without any pre-condition.

The same goes for Dozie. He is loving, hard-working, successful, and only falters once in his life for which he vows he would never forgive himself. Such models of human beings are rare to find in real life. While Ije is too simple, too good to be true, Virginia is too ebullient, too wicked, too inconsiderate, too shameless to be true, either. She should not ever spare herself, for her own wicked nature leads her to tell Dozie that the child she was carrying which allowed her access to his home is someone else's. She carries blackmail to self-destruction.

Other characters as types readily emerge: Patience, the scandal monger; Ugo Ushie the trusted confidante; the mother-in-law, who is too grandchild-crazy to see merit in Ije. All these make the novel read like a morality play where forces of evil defeat themselves and truth emerges triumphant. All the above encumber *Behind the Clouds* and deny it artistic depth.

III

Men Without Ears (Longman, 1984) is a fictive recreation of a sad episode in our national life, especially manifested in the Second Republic with its false fronts, vulgar life-style, ostentatious display of wealth, and sharp business practices. The characters are types rather than sketched in the round: Uloko, the narrator's brother is an ebullient, unscrupulous businessman for whom no holds are barred, thriving in sharp business practices and solicitors of a false front (as a wealthy man). He is closely paralleled by Young Millionaire and most of the other men and women are parvenus, going by several aliases suggestive of wealth such as: *Orimili* (the sea that never dries); *Akajiaku* (the hand that makes wealth); *Osisi na ami ego* (the tree that bears money as its fruits); cash madam; Bank; Madam True Money, et cetera. Uloko's foil is the narrator. Chigo, who stands out as the lone sane voice in a mad society. His sobriety stands in stark relief to the protagonist in whom is subsumed all the vices for which Nigeria's Second Republic was so notorious. Uloko is the man who, like the proverbial heedless fly that follows the corpse into the grave, insists on pursuing a course that leads to self-destruction, just to keep up with the Joneses and maintain a false show of belonging to the wealthy class. This man who is neck-deep in debt, keeps three expensive cars in the garage, throws expensive parties, borrows money from the bank in order to donate nine thousand Naira to the social club to which he belongs, begins to erect a mighty edifice that he does not need in the village (since they already have a commodious family house), gives an expensive "befitting" burial for his father whom he pointedly neglected to care for all along, and dies of a hypertension-induced coma after failing in the ultimate crime: failing in his attempted ritual murder of Nweke, Chigo's houseboy the knowledge of whose escape triggered off the killing stroke from which Uloko never recovered.

The author succeeds in creating the chaos that was reminiscient of the era under scrutiny. What with the chaos at the tout-infested airports; the shows of wealth; the anti-intellectualism and the downgrading of education ("without money, you're nothing", Uloko tells Chigo, and Young Millionaire crows: "I have made nonsense of education with my success. I stopped at standard six you know"); the ostentatious living; the pre-occupation with money (Uloko's reading is confined to two books: *Easy Way to Riches,* and *How to Be a Millionaire);* the corrupt practices by medical doctors and contractors; the lack of taste by the moneyed class. It is the era of the parvenu: a former pauper suddenly metamorphoses as Prince Aha; a trader suddenly transforms himself into "His Royal Highness" with all the trappings of Royalty — a gold-plated throne and page-boys; a publicity seeking trader takes on the sobriquet of "Youngest Millionnaire". Young University lecturers and medical doctors turn into businessmen displaying bogus name-places ("Chief Dr. Engineer Ozo Kelie" as an example), and ordinary professionals elevate their qualifications into titles (Engineer this, Accountant that). In sum, *Men Without Ears* is a sweeping overview of Nigeria's internal illnesses in the home, in the village, at work, in business circles, in social clubs, at burial ceremonies, et cetera, during the Second Republic.

But the problem with this sweeping exposure by Ifeoma Okoye is the linearity, the lack of subtlety in execution. All the characters are flat, except the narrator who by a marlovian turn-about in the end, tries to be a "man without ears" when he takes refuge in telling lies to the police to protect Uloko's reputation after the Nweke episode. The authorial voice is too insistent, and the theme is not conveyed with any subtle hints. The narrator/author repeats *ad nauseam:*

(1) "I had noticed that what was uppermost in most people's minds, literate and illiterate alike, was making money. I had also noticed that here, it was not the man of character who was greatest of men, but the man of means" (p. 75).

(2) Engineer Akah tells Chigo: "Nobody talks of job satisfaction these days. I need money — without money, you are nothing in this country, and business is the quickest way of making money" (p. 7).

(3) Uloko tells Chigo: "You can't be successful without money. Once you have money everything will be yours, including happiness.

All the above can be taken as the novel's main theme which, as I have hinted earlier, is boldly plastered all over the book. Uloko's unhappy end is properly foreshadowed as both Chigo and his father kept reminding Uloko that the part he had chosen could only lead to self-destruction as it indeed led. Finally, name symbols are significant and strengthen the artistic merits of the book. Uloko symbolises, in Igbo parlance, a man who swallows too huge a lump for his throat resulting in the lump getting stuck there. Engineer Akah is the helping hand (note the boarding pass incident) and Chigozie means "may God bless this one".

Men Without Ears registers a noticeable improvement in the artistic growth of Ifeoma Okoye for, in this novel she has advanced from writing literature for children and adolescents, to addressing more mature minds.

IFEOMA OKOYE

Attended Saint Monica's College, Ogbunike from where she obtained a Teachers' Grade Two Certificate, 1959. Holds B.A.(Hons) English from the University of Nigeria, Nsukka 1977. She taught at Saint Monica's College Ogbunike 1960–1961; and at All Saint's International School, 1962–1967. She was the proprietor of Ideal Nursery School, Enugu, 1971–1974. Married to Mokwugo Okoye, they have five (5) children. Currently, a Senior Lecturer, Department of Mass Communications, IMT, Enugu, Anambra State, Nigeria.

Publications

The Adventures of Tulu the Little Monkey, Enugu: Flora Nwapa,

1980
Eme goes to School, Enugu: Flora Nwapa, 1980
No School for Eze, Enugu: Fourth Dimension, 1980
Only Bread for Eze, Enugu: Fourth Dimension, 1980
The Village Boy, Macmillan, 1981
Behind the Clouds, London: Longman, 1982
Men without Ears, London: Longman, 1984
My Tana Alphabet Book, Enugu: Flora Nwapa
My Animal Colouring Book, Enugu Flora Nwapa Books

Works About Her

Ogbonnaya, Obasi "Discover the simple woman, Ifeoma Okoye, award-winning writer of children's literature", *The Guardian* (Nigeria), Sunday, November 10, 1985 p. 10.

Chapter 4

The Novels of Adaora Ulasi

Dr Yemi I. Mojola

Male writers have blazed the trail in every literary genre and sub-
genre practised so far in Nigeria except one: the detective novel written in English. Contrary to the opinion of certain critics writing on
the detective novel in Nigeria, Adaora Ulasi pioneered detective novel
writing in English and up till now, she remains the only female Nigerian detective novelist. Five novels stand to her credit: *Many Thing
You No Understand* (1970) and its continuation, *Many Thing Begin
for Change* (1971) followed by *The Night Harry Died* (1974). After a
silence of four years, *Who is Jonah?* and *The Man from Sagamu* were
published in 1978. Emphasis on detective work progresses gradually
from the first to the fourth novel which represents the culmination
of her detective writing. The last novel, in our view, appears to be
more of a mystery novel than a detective novel in spite of the strong
presence of the police.

The *Night Harry Died* which occupies a median position in
Ulasi's literary production is the only novel set outside Nigeria. The
plot unfolds in a small town in the State of Louisiana in the South of
the United States of America at the beginning of the twentieth century in a conservative society. *Many Thing You No Understand* and
Many Thing Begin for Change are set in the Igbo-speaking areas of
Eastern Nigeria in 1935 right in the heat of colonisation. *Who is
Jonah?* is set in South-Eastern Nigeria during the latter part of the
colonial era as can be deduced from the presence of white people in
key positions of responsibility. *The Man From Sagamu*, as the title
suggests, takes place in Sagamu, a town in Western Nigeria, a reference to human sacrifices being "in the early fifties", "thing of the past
for nearly fifty years" situates the novel in the early part of the nine-
teen-fifties.

Setting literary works within well-defined spatial and temporal
dimensions imposes on the author a concern for accuracy in the presentation of cultural, social and situational realities if and when they
feature in the works. This, however, is not always the case in the
novels under consideration. For example, in *Many Thing Begin for*

Change, and anachronistic description is given of Amaku, a town located in the hinterland in Eastern Nigeria. It is described as being, in 1935, a town with "heavy industries", a town where the "arrival of foreign investors and the industrial complexities they created" changed the "pure and simple" "African township", a town whose elite took delight in spending its

> "evenings at each others' homes, splicing the rounds of brandy and soda with fond recollections of their student days in lodings in Fulham, Camden Town and Notting Hill Gate, and of their Sunday afternoons in Hyde Park listening to the speakers on their soap boxes" *(Many Thing Begin for Change,* p. 67)

In the same novel, the level of sophistication in the production of the newspaper, *The Daily Observer,* the highly advanced organisational capability of its publishers, the expertise of its journalists in investigative journalism, though a laudable witness to the author's knowledge of the internal activities of a newspaper house, represent historical inaccuracies for certainly in 1935, a hinterland town such as Amaku could not have had a newspaper, how much more a highly advanced one! The author's familiarity with western society must have influenced her vision of Nigerian realities in her artistic creations thus giving rise to such incongruities as the above example occurring in a society which still demands the burial of twenty human heads with a dead Obi.

A case of direct misinformation about cultural realities occurs in Adaora Ulasi's conception of Sagamu in *The Man From Sagamu* as a town which celebrates with pomp "the famous yearly Oshun Festival which lasts for a week". The novelist amply describes imagined preparations for and the celebration of the festival whereas, in reality, the Oshun festival takes place annually in Oshogbo and never in Sagamu.

The major theme running through the novels, although in varying degrees, is that of crime and detection. Its best expression is found in *Who is Jonah?* in *Many Thing You No Understand* and *The Man From Sagamu,* other preoccupations are evident. In the latter, attention is centred on myth and superstition, traditional beliefs and practices, and the celebration of the Oshun festival by the people of Sagamu whose peace a most unsociable and unloved citizen of the town, Olu Agege, disturbs by deliberately disappearing just before the festival. The constant references to the mystery surrounding Agege's birth, to his life-style and his knowledge of black magic as well as his ghostly appearances to various people on different occasions tilt this novel towards the mystery novel.

From the mysterious circumstances superstitiously believed to have surrounded Agege's birth and from subsequent references to his unusual situation, it appears that Agege's earthly sojourn is for the fulfilment of a mission. It is only at the very end of the novel that the mission comes to light when he explains that he is "the reincarnation in human form of the Oshun Deity". A not too convincing explanation when one recalls that Agege had to exert himself to learn the art of black magic: "he had concentrated with singular attention in the learning of this art, especially the illusionary part of it" so "that he could make any thing he wished to vanish, and was later to make those who saw it believe it whole-heartedly". *(The Man From Sagamu,* p.24) The reincarnation of a deity should not need to strive to acquire such extraordinary skills for he belongs to the realm of the supernatural; they should be natural to him.

The 'messianic' role of being "a living sacrifice" which Oladele Taiwo *(Female Novelists of Modern Africa,* p.99) ascribes to Agege is far-fetched for it is out of tune with his character of general unfriendliness to all except to children to whom he distributes coins occasionally, the only occasions "that he had human contact, if one could call it that." On the spur of the moment, his disappearance of his own volition constitutes a relief to others who have come to regard him as a "cross . . . they had had to bear". However, when its implication becomes known in view of the approaching Oshun Festival, the whole town, the Oba more than all others, is disturbed. Meanwhile, Agege feels self-satisfied over his disappearance and laughs "himself hoarse" in his hiding-place at the rumours circulating about his movements and at the inability of the town's leading seer and police to locate him. A man with a mission of self-sacrifice on behalf of his people would not cause deliberate pandemonium and encourage more superstitious beliefs among the very people he wishes to save "from their supertitious beliefs and ritual worship" (Oladele Taiwo, *loc. cit).* That "there would never be another festival like the one that was about to take place" does not mean that Agege is making a "once-for-all sacrifice" rendering "no other sacrifice . . . necessary". It is obvious that an Olu Agege, having revealed himself as the reincarnation of the Oshun Deity, after his final disappearance, would never again deliberately disappear just before the Oshun Festival thus creating a dilemma for the whole town and making that particular festival extraordinary.

On the other hand; in *Many Thing You No Understand,* a cultural and judicial confrontation between traditional Igbo authority and colonial authority underscoring a low-keyed tussle for political power appears to be the thematic focus although its treatment is rather pedestrian. The confrontation stems from the traditional demand of burying twenty human heads with a dead Obi, a requirement which was met at the death of Chief Obieze II of Ukana. The incident would have gone undetected by the colonial administration but for the complaint lodged by a non-native of Ukana, Sylvester Udu, whose brother's head rounded up the grisky collection of heads to the Assistant District Officer (A.D.O.) John Macintosh, who then decides to investigate the matter. With great reluctance Maurice Mason, the District Officer (D.O.), collaborates with his A.D.O. in the investigation for he repeatedly insists on avoiding confrontation by not interfering with local customs. It is therefore inconsistent with his attitude that immediately after the sudden repatriation of the A.D.O. due to a medically inexplicable illness, Mason, without any necessity to modify his position, decides to pursue the investigation actively, a decision which leads directly to his being ambushed at the end of the novel.

Many Thing Begin For Change opens with the murder of Mason thus constituting a follow-up of the first novel. Its main plot is based on the search for Mason and the perpetrators of the crime. Although an obvious link exists between the two novels in terms of space, time, plot and characters, the British colonial administration is portrayed in the first novel as disorganised, incompetent and generally pleasure-loving but in the second novel, the same administration exhibits cohesion, competence and a sense of purpose. Such a contradiction is artistically unconvincing although it might be argued that in the colonialists' view, the situation in the second novel is more compelling since it involves the death of one of them. If the two novels are seen as a pair, *Many Thing You No Understand* can be regarded as the peparation for the actual detective work undertaken in *Many Thing Begin For Change*. However, if the first novel is considered in isolation, one has the impression that in its conception and realisation, the writer was not yet sure of her vocation for the novel stands as a weak expression of the conflict between traditional and colonial authorities as well as of detective novel writing for the detective intention becomes unmistakable only in the second novel.

All the novels, apart from *Many Thing Begin For Change* and *The Night Harry Died,* comprise simple unique plots with a linear chronological development. In the former novel, another plot in which a coal-miner is murdered and the suspect commits suicide develops about one-third of the way through the narration. It is linked to the original plot by District Commissioner Hughes' discovery that the Secret Society headed by Obieze III, who finally commits suicide, has been responsible for the ambush and death of Mason as well as for other atrocities such as the murder of the miner. In the latter novel, too many twists arising from mistaken identities complicate the plot. In fact, at the denouement, the reader is not absolutely sure of what has transpired. This is because Harry Collier, the central male character, contradicts his earlier account of how his half-brother to whom he bears a very close resemblance, had replaced him for nine months as a sick husband nursed by his wife, Edna. As Willfred Feuser aptly sums up the situation, the "intrigue is encumbered by an overuse of the doppelganger motif".

The plot of the detective novel must be ingenuously constructed to create continuous tension and excitement in order to arouse and retain the interest of the reader and ensure his collaboration through the use of suspense and surprise, especially. In *Many Thing You No Understand and Many Thing Begin For Change,* the elements of suspense and surprise are almost absent due to the technical error of identifying the culprits and their motives at the beginning of the narration. In *The Man From Sagamu,* the narrator explains, barely twenty pages into the narration, that Agege's disappearance is due to his knowledge of black magic. The reader knows his hiding-place, all his preparations for his few days' sojourn there, his actions, thoughts and reactions to the search for him. Only his motive for this disruptive disappearance remains to be discovered, an aspect which is emphasised in the narration.

However, in *The Night Harry Died,* Harry Collier's appearance at his own funeral thus throwing the small town of Alligator Creek into utter confusion and consternation due especially to the impossibility of arresting Harry's ubiquitous and supposedly violent ghost, creates tension. The reader is anxious to discover the truth about Harry: how did sand replace his corpse in the coffin? Is his ghost really roaming about with destruction in its wake? These and several other questions throng the reader's mind.

In *Who is Jonah?,* the elements of suspense, surprise and drama heighten the curiosity and anxiety of the reader. Hardly has the multilated body of Frobisher, the dubious white man, who made his living by selling "chunky trinkets" and showing silent films in different localities been deposited in the mortuary than it is stolen. The police soon discover the body of a woman with a two months old pregnancy in Frobisher's travelling van. With one surprising discovery following another at well-timed intervals, tension gradually builds up. The climax comes with the police's conclusion that the innocent looking nurse, Joseph Osakwe, alias Jonah Joseph Isu, on whose innocence the white doctor, Conningham, has so often insisted, is the culprit aided by his father, Hezekiah, the head-hunter. The disappearance of Joseph and his father, already arrested by the police, right in the presence of the police chief and his assistants, constitutes an anticlimax in surprise. What we find technically problematic in the plot of this novel is the rationally unexplained manner in which Chief Inspector Nze arrives at determining Joseph's guilt.

It is only in *Who is Jonah?* that a well-qualified personnel conducts the investigation and this explains the professionally methodical search for the culprits and the establishment of the motives for the crimes. In the other novels, various categories of people, an overwhelming majority untrained in criminal investigation, participate in the search for the offenders, a situation which detracts from the quality of the works as detective novels. In *Many Thing You No Understand*, British colonial civil servants, in *Many Thing Begin For Change*, still colonial administrators and a journalist, undertake the investigation. In *The Night Harry Died*, it is the sheriff and the townspeople and in *The Man From Sagamu*, the police and the whole town, all terrified by the very "people" for whom they are searching. While the lack of professionalism already dooms the outcome of their search, the real source of their inability to find their targets lies in the concept of "flesh and blood" people searching for a ghost in *The Night Harry Died* and for an unusual mysterious character who publicly vanishes into thin air "at 3 p.m." in *The Man From Sagamu.*

An interesting and innovative aspect of Ulasi's works is the consistent introduction of African mysticism into her Nigeria-based novels, an aspect which reflects a reality not only Nigerian but also African. In *The Man From Sagamu*, Adaora Ulasi devotes a long paragraph to explaining the absolute importance of black magic in Africa. "There isn't a single country in the whole of the African continent where the inhabitants are free from black magic" *(The Man From Sagamu, p.24)*, she affirms. Its inclusion in various forms in her works is thus a deliberate attempt at reflecting a well-known socio-cultural reality.

In *Many Thing You No Understand*, black magic *(juju)* serves as a means to launch a counter-attack on those responsible for reducing Chukwuka and Okafor, the elders charged with the traditional responsibility for collecting the twenty heads, to wanted persons whose movements are curtailed. One of the elders attacks the complainant, Sylvester Udu, by employing "juju" to "scatter" his brain so that he becomes insane and gives a contradictory account of his original complaint. A venomous snake, sent to poison the A.D.O., does not succeed in its deadly mission and so they strike him with a medically inexplicable hallucinatory disease thus forcing his repatriation. In *Who is Jonah?*, Hezekiah, the head-hunter, casts a spell on the white

Commissioner of Police incapacitating him for a while.

The traditional method of crime detection and discovering the unknown comes into play in *The Man From Sagamu* in which the Oba invites the town's leading seer, Baba Kekere, to locate Agege through his magical powers. He fails because Agege's knowledge of black magic surpasses his own knowledge. Consulting seers for the resolution of the varied and innumerable problems of existence cuts across national, ethnic and religious boundaries even in contemporary African societies.

A third aspect of the use of black magic is what we have termed the 'disappearance device'. In *Who is Jonah?*, the Isus escape justice by disappearing, a feat which baffles the Commissioner of Police so much that he exclaims to Chief Inspector Nze, who is equally bewildered, "Explain it to me . . . because I can't understand it". *The Man From Sagamu*, of course, centres around Agege's disappearance in broad daylight. He later on assumes different shapes on his ghostly visits to Magistrate Adewunmi and the Oba. One could in fact surmise that it is he that appears to Peter Jones, the white Resident Officer at Ijebu-Ode, in the form of "the strangest-looking beast he had ever seen", and animal with "the head of a deer but its body had spots like a leopard." The conspicuous presence of the supernatural, the suggestions of ritualism and the featuring of hair-raising, spine-chilling incidents confer a strong flavour of mystery on Ulasi's works.

All social classes, from traditional rulers, passing through white colonial civil service and police chiefs to servants, people Ulasi's fictional universe. The novelist generally depicts her characters through their actions and reactions and reduces physical and moral descriptions to an outline in one or two sentences. All the central characters are men except in *The Night Harry Died* where Edna, who has been subjected to mental, sexual and financial exploitation by her husband, becomes an accused and eventually a convict for attempted murder. Apart from an inconsequential role as a telephone operator played by a young lady in *Many Thing Begin For Change* and a victim's role, a minor role played by another woman in *Who is Jonah?*, women, black or white, feature only as housewives acting as moral support and counsellors to their husbands at periods of crises. The detective nature of the novels may explain in part the relegation of women to the background for in reality, women are less involved in the commission and detection of crime than men. It is also a direct reflection of the role of women in most traditional societies.

The image cut by colonial administrators especially in *Many Thing You No Understand* leaves much to be desired. For example, from his discussions and actions, from his advice to his A.D.O.,

Macintosh, and from the opinion of some of his colleagues, one would assume that taking indigenous women to bed constitutes Mason's paramount interest. And the A.D.O. himself, who appears to be morally sound, is revealed, eventually, as possessing homosexual propensities. The most senior colonial officers are also depicted as bossy, arrogant and sometimes cruel. District Commissioner Hughes in the same novel and its continuation as well as the Commissioner of Police, MacIntyre, in *Who is Jonah?* often take pleasure in mentally torturing their immediate subordinates through humiliating them and engaging them in endless squabbles. An overt distrust also exists between them and the white doctors heading the hospitals. It is only in *The Man From Sagamu* that the white Resident Officer for Sagamu Division has a more humane personality. The general negative depiction of these colonial officers would suggest a desire to satirise the colonial administration, but for the absence of the usual tools of satire.

An extensive use of dialogue which gives the effect of rapidity in the development of the narrations characterizes some of Ulasi's works, *Who is Jonah?* in particular. In an attempt to indicate either the stark illiteracy or the semi-illiteracy of some of her characters, the novelist adopts pidgin English as their medium of expression. While she expertly handles standard English, her effort at using pidgin English miscarries because of her lack of a thorough knowledge of it. Consequently, in the four novels of Nigerian inspiration, the poor quality of the pidgin English detracts from the aesthetic effect and thereby lessens the entertainment value of the works.

The situation is further compounded by the unnecessary and undesirable use of pidgin English where standard English would have been more appropriate. For example, even though the Yoruba never use pidgin English as a means of communication among themselves, the Oba of Sagamu addresses not only his subjects but also his senior wife in pidgin English, an impossible occurrence in contemporary Yoruba society, much less in the early fifties. Even in the societies where pidgin English is commonly used, among the Igbos for example, one would not expect the ordinary Igbo man of the 1930s to communicate with his people through this medium. But, Chief Obieze in 1935 discusses state matters with the two elders, Chukwuka and Okafor, in pidgin English and carries on intimate conversations with his favourite wife in the same idiom.

However, in the novel set in the United States, *The Night Harry Died,* the adoption of the local American version of the English language in appropriate circumstances enhances the use of language in the novel. In spite of certain inconsistencies in speeches by the same characters under the same conditions, the novelist successfully reflects the language situation of the society by making her less educated characters use the local idiom. A conscious effort to arouse laughter is observable in the exchanges between the characters but the attempt sometimes falls flat and is unconvincing such as when Harry Collier publicly insults the judge in court by referring to his lowly family antecedents.

A feature of Ulasi's works is the presence of identical characteristics in several respects. For example, Hughes in *Many Thing You No Understand* closely resembles MacIntyre in *Who is Jonah?* in their negative character traits. Harry Collier in *The Night Harry Died* has his counterpart in Olu Agege in *The Man From Sagamu* — unloved, unsociable, fear-inducing and mystery — clad men who force their respective societies to reckon with them. Arguments between colonial heads of administration or the police and their immediate white assistants are prominent in *Many Thing You No Understand, Many Thing Begin For Change* and *Who is Jonah?* In three of the novels, court cases feature; of course, the disappearance feats in two of the novels come to mind. Do these parallels indicate sterility in ideas and imagination?

Whatever the reservations one may have about the quality of Adaora Ulasi's novels, her major contribution to Nigerian literature lies in her pioneering the writing of detective novels in English. Her best effort in this respect, *Who is Jonah?* merits serious consideration. The consistent introduction of marvellous realism *a l'africaine* into her works, thereby recreating in fiction a living aspect of the African cultural heritage which most educated people pretend to be an illusion in public, but embrace in the privacy of their conscience, is remarkable. Ulasi has been silent for over seven years. It is our hope that her long silence is not indicative of insufficient or dried-up inspiration but of further maturation in preparing for subsequent literary production.

ADAORA LILY ULASI

Born at Aba in 1932 by an Igbo Chief from the Royal House of Nnewi. Studied journalism first at Pepperdine University and then at the University of Southern California, Los Angeles, where she obtained a B.A. degree. Was a Women's Page Editor of both the *Daily Times* and *Sunday Times* (Nigeria) in the sixties; Editor, *Woman's World,* 1972. The circulation of the latter "more than tripled under her editorship as she expanded its interests to include news of the achievements of women in Nigeria and around the world". Has done radio work for *The Voice of America*. Writes for the Nigerian *Daily Star*. Currently lives in England where she has been since 1967. Has three-children.

Publication

Many Thing You No Understand, London: Michael Joseph, 1970.
Many Thing Begin for Change, London: Michael Joseph, 1971.
The Night Harry Died, (1974).
Who is Jonah? Ibadan: Onibonoje Press, 1978.
The Man From Sagamu, Glasgow: Fontana Collins, 1978.

Works About Her

Taiwo Oladele, 'Adaora Lily Ulasi' in *Female Novelists of Modern Africa*, London: Macmillan, 1984 pp. 84—99.

Chapter 5

The Ascetic Feminist Vision of Zaynab Alkali

Seiyifa Koroye

The general feeling in Nigerian literary circles is that the publication of *The Stillborn* marks the birth of a major new talent. The popular press was still busy welcoming the author, Zaynab Alkali, as one of the first female writers to emerge from Northern Nigeria when the novel won the prestigious Association of Nigerian Authors (ANA) prize for prose fiction in 1985. Such high acclaim calls for a dispassionate, critical assessment of the novel. In what, precisely, does the promise of this first novel lie?

The answer may be summarised thus: Mrs. Alkali's subject is (perhaps, predictably) woman, but her treatment of it indicates a remarkably new emphasis which is different in degree, if not in kind, from the feminist positions made familiar by novelists like Flora Nwapa and Buchi Emecheta. An ascetic vision of the truly liberated woman informs the theme as well as the style of *The Stillborn*. There is hardly a trace of excess of self-indulgence in Mrs Alkali's prose; and this austere style effectively underscores the central argument of the novel. For the image of the new woman — not a stillbirth, but a fully formed, independent person — that *The Stillborn* presents is inscribed all over with the ascetic ideals of 'determination' and 'virtue': roles and identity allotted a woman by a male-dominated society; and virtue in being able at the same time to forgive and redeem the man or men in her life who cannot, it seems, desist from inflicting on her the most vicious forms of oppression and brutalisation.

Li, for "short Libira — needle" (p.5), is an embodiment of this new image. She bears on her thin frame a huge burden of aborted dreams until she is able, at thirty, to resolve to dream dreams that "would not be stillborn" (p.105). There are two sub-plots, involving Awa and Faku, Li's elder sister and friend, respectively, which accentuate the poignancy of the theme of shattered illusions. The three young women are all traumatised by their marriages as each husband turns out to be not quite the right choice. The husbands are seen to be, in their different ways, both unloving and unlovable. Only Li, however, realises at the end that her husband, Habu, has seemed un-

lovable precisely because he has not been the dream lover her childhood desires decorated so elaborately with illusion.

The narrative opens on the day Li returns to the village after
completing her primary education at a boarding school. She is thirteen, and yearns to escape from the suffocating atmosphere of a
_ home – she calls it "worse than a prison" (p.3) – presided over by
an unloving and domineering father, assisted by an equally unpleasant deaf mother. "She felt *trapped and unhappy.* . . . she missed the
kind of life she had lived at the primary boarding school, *free and
gay*" (p.3, emphases mine). Freedom and gaiety: these desires
suddenly seem fulfillable when she meets Habu Adams at a village
dance which, (to attend, she had crept through an opening in the fen-
ce late in the night to avoid detection by her father). Habu, handsome
and flamboyant, talks of leaving home soon to train as a doctor. Two
years later, at fifteen, Li marries him just before he leaves for the
city: The dream of escape and happiness, fuelled these two years past
by her daring trysts with Habu in a village that disapproves of such
things, is about to be fulfilled: "the qualified doctor, the Grade I teacher, the big European house full of servants, the smooth body, the
long silk hair . . . There was no end to the luxuries the city could
offer." (p.57).

Li does indeed become a Grade I teacher – fifteen years later –
and even then, only as a result of the search for a balm for the
wounds caused by splinters from her exploded dreams. Her first disappointment is that, in the city, Habu has "become a salesman
instead of a doctor" (p.57). Secondly, for all of four years, he has
not fulfilled his promise to ask her to join him in the city. Fresh
suitors – chief amongst them, the wealthy Alhaji Bature – pester
her: she has become an abandoned wife. When, finally, she is taken
to Habu by a relative of his, "Li knew she had lost her man to the
city" (p.70). Shortly after her arrival, Habu goes out; he does not
return until nightfall the day after, "drunk and violent"; and it is in
"the drunken intimacy" (p.70) that ensures – the first and the last in
the city – that he impregnates her. Heavy with child, burdened with
the bitter nightly knowledge that "the man lying on the other side of
the room was a well-dressed stranger who did not talk to a village
woman" (p.70), Li readily takes the news of her father's illness as an
opportunity to return to the village.

She arrives home to find that Baba has already been buried, but
this loss strikes her with far less force than the living death that
marriage has turned out to be for her friend, Faku. Li, spending the
night in Kano with Faku on her way to the village, finds her friend
faring very badly as Garba's second wife. Garba, city-slicker on a visit

to the village, was to Faku what Habu was to Li: the man who would take the little girl away from the prison and poverty of village life. The two pairs of lovers, together with the pair of Dan Fiama, village headmaster, and Awa, got married at about the same time. Now, almost six years after they went their different ways, Li knocks on Garba's door, wondering what Faku would look like: "Fat? Modern looking? Rich and sophisticated? Li had learnt from Faku's mother.,, that Garba had another woman with six children. How did they all live?" (p.76). The plump village girl has become "a thin haggard" woman: "How could this near-stranger be her friend, Faku? Famished in body and, no doubt, famished in soul?" (p.76). Faku reports that she does not see her husband often. Of the senior wife, married twenty years with nine children (three more have been born since Faku's mother last heard from Kano), Faku says: "She is the mother-of-the-house and the master of the house too" (p.79). In two dreams that night, Li confirms, through symbolic representations, the bitter import of her meeting with Faku: "Li had felt cold and lonely, but here was someone who she sensed felt much colder and lonelier" (p.79). She senses that Garba no longer sleeps with Faku (she still has only one child, conceived in the days of village courtship) and also that Faku is conscious of and yet unable to do anything about the futility and horror of her marriage. And so:

> In the morning, . . . she asked her friend once more if she had told her everything about her marriage and if she was truly happy.
> By God, I am enjoying my life in the city! Isn't the city what you and I always wanted . . .?" Faku said vehemently.
> By my ancestors, yes, but I am talking about you, not the city," Li replied. Faku avoided her friend's eyes. (p. 80).

This is the turning point for Li: the point at which the spirit of independence she has shown since her childhood assumes the form of a steely, feminist determination to rely, not on a husband, but on herself for the fulfilment of her dreams.

When next we see Li (chapter 8), she is already twenty-nine. Armed with virtue and determination, she successfully resists the advances of fresh suitors and completes her studies at teachers' college. She also refuses to go back to Habu, although the latter has visited her twice at school and sent friends to plead for a reconciliation.

Li's triumph — almost an apotheosis — is the subject of the Epilogue. When their grandfather dies, Awa tells Li: "The mourners are outside and waiting for you. You are the man of the house now" (p.101). And then the narrator comments:

> Li ought to have felt fulfilled, but instead she felt empty. It wasn't just the emptiness of bereavement, but an emptiness that went beyond that. For ten years she had struggled towards certain goals. Now, having accomplished these goals, she wished there was something else to struggle for. For that was the only way life could be meaningful. (p.102).

She falls into a reverie, during which she sees her great-grand-daughter getting married and advises her against the false consciousness that romantic illusions can induce in women: "Don't be like me. I spent my entire life dreaming. I forgot to live'" (p.104). Yet she is able to tell the young woman: "'I have never been alone. I have Habu Adams'" (p.104). When she awakens, therefore, to hear her ten-year-old daughter Shuwa ask whether she was dreaming about her father, Habu, Li is surprised: Awa, with whom Shuwa lived while Li was away at college had been under instructions not to tell the child anything about her father. Li "knew now that the bond that had tied her to the father of her child was not ruptured" (pp.104—105).

As the novel ends, Li is about to return to Habu in the city:

> "Why, Li? The man is lame", said the sister.
> "We are all lame, daughter-of-my-mother. But this is not time to crawl. It is time to learn to walk again".
> "So you want to hold the crutches and lead the way?" Awa asked.
> "No", answered Li.
> "What then, you want to walk behind and arrest his fall?"
> "No, I will just hand him the crutches and side by side we will learn to walk". (p. 105).

Habu is still in hospital with crushed legs following a motor accident. When we first learn about the accident, Li is explaining to her sister that Habu seems to have "lost the will to live'", for "'the doctors say they have done everything that they can, and that the rest depends on him'" (pp.92—93). So Li is returning now in the knowledge that she is going to help Habu regain the will to live. Having purged herself of false expectations and having demonstrated that she can achieve great things without using her husband as a crutch (i.e., once she has disburdened herself of romantic dreams), she undertakes to make whole again a man broken in body as well as spirit.

Wiry and tough-minded, undefeated though brutalised, Li emerges as the model of the heroic and truly liberated woman Mrs. Alkali clearly sets out to celebrate, and to whom the tough but old-fashioned Awa and the weak and vapid Faku stand as foils in their different ways.

ZAYNAB ALKALI

Born 3 February, 1950 of the Tura Muslim group who presently live in Dan Mirnga, among the plains of Biu in Borno State. She was educated at Waka Girl's Primary School, Biu, 1961—63; Queen Elizabeth Secondary School, Ilorin, Kwara State, 1964—1968 and Bayero University, Kano, 1969—73 where she obtained a B.A. degree in English. Taught at School of Arabic Studies, Kano. Principal Shekara Girl's Boarding School, Kano, 1974—1976; Assistant Lecturer/M.A. student, Bayero University, Kano, 1976—1979; Lecturer in English and African Literature, University of Maiduguri, Borno State, 1980—1984. Currently, Senior Lecturer in English and Co--ordinator of English and General Studies, Modibbo Adama College, University of Maiduguri, Yola Campus. Married in 1971 to Dr Mohammed Nur Alkali, Vice-Chancellor, University of Maiduguri. They have five children.

Publications

The Stillborn, (Drumbeat) Longman, 1984
The Virtuous Woman. (Gong Series) Ikeja, Longman 1985/86
The Cobwebs. (unpublished)

Works about Her

The Stillborn. Reviewed in *Sunday New Nigerian,* Sunday, 12 January, 1986, by Bamikunle, Aderemi
An interview, by Odia Ofeimun, *The Guardian,* Wednesday, 27 March 1985.

II

The Dramatists

Chapter 6

The Nigerian Woman as a Dramatist: The Instance of Tess Onwueme

Dr Chidi Amuta

The growth of Nigerian literature can now be conceived of in more than statistical terms. There has occurred, especially in the period since after the Nigerian Civil War (1967–70), a great diversification in Nigerian literature both in terms of the world-view, class, origins and geo-political distribution of writers. This development, which is a logical consequence of the relative explosion in social development in the decade of the 1970s, has also been characterised by an unprecedented awakening of political consciousness both among the writers as well as in their Nigerian target audience. A significant component of the development in question is the increase in the number of women writers with the result that what used to be a minority tradition with only such names as Flora Nwapa and Mabel Segun has recently blossomed into a rich harvest boasting such relatively successful writers as Ifeoma Okoye, Zaynab Alkali, Buchi Emecheta, Zulu Sofola and Tess Onwueme.

Onwueme's fledgling importance in this tradition can be attributed to her relative youth (aged about 32 years), her ability to write, direct and produce her own plays as well as a certain incipient rebelliousness in her works which marks her apart from most of her compeers. For one thing, Onwueme's art has not been circumscribed by the fact of her being a woman. In other words, her thematic fixation has not merely been conditioned by the fashionable stance of "presenting the female angle" but rather a more liberal approach of focusing attention on topical issues in the contemporary Nigerian (and African) Society. This is perhaps her way of contending that the African woman writer, like her male counterparts, is a member of a specific society whose experiences are conditioned by broad problems and issues that do not often discriminate between the sexes. More importantly, Onwueme would appear to have carved an additional niche for herself in Nigerian literature by contributing to a gradual tilting of the geo-political disequilibrium in the distribution of genres. There has, until lately, been a dominance of the drama scene in Nigeria by Yoruba male playwrights while the arena of prose fiction (especially the novel form) has tended to be dominated by the Igbos. Onwueme's emergence as a dramatist of growing national importance, given her Igbo ethnic origins, thus becomes additionally significant, in the larger equation in Nigerian literature.

Born at Ogwashi-Uku in Bendel State, Onwueme has managed to combine her roles as wife, mother and teacher with the more onerous one of playwright. The fruits of her endeavour include about seven plays: *The Broken Calabash* (Totan, 1984), *A Hen Too Soon* (Heins, 1983); *The Desert Encroaches;* (Totan, 1985); *A Scent of Onions; Faces of a Coin; Our Son Tom;* and *De Governor.* Tess Onwueme also has a volume of yet unpublished poems to her credit. Of her plays, two titles can be said to account for her growing reputation: *The Broken Calabash,* a film version of which was aired by the NTA on national network as part of Nigeria's Silver Jubilee Celebration and *The Desert Encroaches,* which won the Association of Nigerian Authors (ANA) prize for drama in 1985. It is also from these two works that the essence of Onwueme's sensibility and dramatic method to date can be distilled.

The Broken Calabash takes as its thematic province the rather familiar subject of the clash or conflict between the values, institutions and practices of old Africa and those attendant on the growing westernisation of the African. This theme should be familiar to those who are conversant with the beginnings of the literary tradition in African drama in general. It is the concern in such early plays as Soyinka's *The Lion and the Jewel,* Kobina Sekyi's *The Blinkards* and James Ene Henshaw's *This is Our Chance.* What Onwueme brings to this theme is a certain sense of contemporaneity which pitches the conflicts in the context of present-day Africa with its universities and other modern institutions. Thus, Ona, the heroine is a university undergraduate. She would like to marry Diaku, a man of her choice according to the dictates of western romance. But as an only child of her parents, she is an *Idegbe,* which implies that she must marry from her family and procreate within it in order to maintain the purity of her family's blood. To compound her case, Diaku, her loved one, is an *Osu* — a member of a group of outcast that should be familiar to those who have read Achebe's *No Longer at Ease* and *Things Fall Apart.* Her father, Courtuma, insists that tradition be upheld while Ona would prefer to have her way in line with the changing times. This conflict, at first domestic and filial, graduates into metaphysical proportions as it comes to symbolise the conflict of will between two antithetical cultural values — the one receding and stubborn, and the other, equally strong and growing.

At first, there would appear to be an underlying conflict at the emotional level between Diaku and Courtuma for Ona's affection. But Courtuma's relationship with his daughter has something of an incestuous streak about it with him thinking of and talking to his daughter in terms overloaded with Freudian overtones.

Ona: Papa, you must let me go. Otherwise, I can't receive holy communion on Sunday.

Courtuma: .....Don't let it bother you. I brew the best palm-wine in Isah and we can buy biscuits to..... White man's communion? I have seen that cassock my dear child, and I can show that what that priest has in them I have too. If he, another man, can forgive sin and hold you captive with his biscuits and wine, what wonder would the power of juice from — from a loving father not? (pp. 32 — 33).

Consequently, Courtuma's possessive attitude towards Ona derives from a combination of fidelity to tradition and a certain subdued libidinal impulse. He invokes tradition to frustrate Ona's desires and in the process compels Diaku to marry Ego, one of Ona's friends. The injured Ona wreaks vengeance on her possessive father by accusing him of the responsibility for her pregnancy. Caught in the pangs of shame and indignation, Courtuma commits suicide. This tragic ending is celebrated in the play as a victory for modernity albeit a blood-stained victory, a way of illustrating the truism that socio-cultural change is inevitably a contradictory process:

The moon is full, the old season dies.
A new crop is sown.
What harvest do you foresee? Today is the climax of the festival ending the drudgery of the old season.
The new yam will be eaten but it is streaked with blood..... (p. 27).

The Desert Encroaches extends Onwueme's thematic horizon beyond the bounds of the ethnic world. Here, she takes as her subject the growing arms race among the super-powers and also the increasing polarization of the world into East and West, North and South. Through an essentially allegorical strategy, this play brings together representatives of these various geo-political and ideological formations into a grand summit of assorted beasts. Each zone strives to legitimise its viewpoint and attempts to institute dialogue which produces only a tradition of "holding talks" while the world burns and "the desert encroaches."

What this play laments is the increasing desiccation of humanity, our morality and sensitivity as well as the imminence of disaster attendant on the growing arms race. Excerpts:

Tortoise:	Do you see the cauldron in the West? Animals, can you feel thunder corked in a bottle on heat? Nuclear germ pre-seed, planted and poised to wipe us all in a batting of the eye..... Why must they burn MILLIONS.....BILLIONS.....and TRILLIONS on the atomic cauldron?
Dog:	While the earth starves. While we long for our throats to be irritated.....
Narrator:	A boil swells in the bowel of the earth. Each day, it ripens ..... Do you wish to stand and see it burst..... Do you?

This is essentially a moralistic play, intent on cajoling a world divided into opposing camps and governed by rugged and aggressive economic and ideological motivations to accept a common morality that would banish the instruments for the acquisition and retention of power.

More directly relevant, however, is the insight which this play provides into the relations among members of the various opposing and contending regions and power blocs. It is unsparing in its indictment of Third World leaders for their quisling and powerless compromise with the developed economies — just as it condemns the big powers for their senseless worship of the instruments of death.

Tortoise:	But all the fault is not theirs. Are they not aided by sons of our land to manipulate us? Our dogs are servile. They bark and bark at the moon, at us and threaten the wind — their brethren with their growl but to the master they wag their tail — As the masters eat. They stoop and observe the movement from hand to mouth..... (pp. 32/33).

At the level of artistry, Onwueme is first and foremost a symbolist dramatist. She exploits the immense power of symbolism, the ability to use the particular to mediate the general in order to elevate her drama above the merely literal and specific levels. In *The Broken Calabash*, for instance, the central symbol, which also embodies the Diaku's parents to ask for Ona's hand in marriage which Courtuma central thematic contention, is the calabash of palm-wine brought by breaks in a fit of rage. This physical breaking of the calabash symbolises both Ona's shattered emotional aspiration and stability as well as the tradition which Courtuma strives so hard to protect and defend. This act of hubris evokes a historic question which summarises the theme of the play in question: " ..... how do you think you can save our tradition by breaking another?"

Similarly in *The Desert Encroaches*, the various formations — socio-economic and ideological — the global political equation are represented by various animal figures: the lion for the United States and the Bear for the Soviet Union. The Hyena and the Wolf are similarly linked with the West just as the Fox is assortment of beasts ranging from Ant, Cow, Old Donkey to Dog, Sheep, etc. The artistic strength of this play thus derives from the playwright's ability to match the specific natural attributes of the different animals with the political, economic and ideological idiosyncracies of those parts of the world they are created to represent. It is perhaps the sheer bestiality of international politics that is being lampooned.

In terms of dramatic method, Onwueme displays a high degree of innovativeness and great technical variability. From the fairly straightforward ritualistic form of *The Broken Calabash,* we get a fairly highly involved drama in *The Desert Encroaches.* If the former play reminds us of Efua Sutherland, the latter contains echoes of Brecht through Osofisan. There is here the attempt at dispelling the illusion of reality through the introduction of a director who introduces both the actors and the subject of the play. There is also the rapid switches from one movement to the next as well as the anti-illusionary technique of making human characters engage in the make-belief that they are acting animals.

A fair assessment of this young playwright's achievement to date cannot but end on a tentative note. Her vision is still evolving; so also is her technique. There is still in her work a certain amateurish handling of metaphor as well as a striving for linguistic authenticity which require time to season into a distinctive idiom of expression. There is also a disturbing simplicity in her grasp of the issues which constitute her themes. A case in point is her reductionist moralistic handling of the rather complex issue of big power relationships in *The Desert Encroaches.* In spite of an essentially idealistic articulation of the theme in the main body of the play, the ending suggests a certain confidence in the power of the down-trodden, echoing an apparent leftist inclination even after condemning both capitalism and socialism in the earlier parts of the play.

It needs to be conceded, in conclusion, that with Onwueme, one is dealing with a creative imagination that is quite fertile and which holds out a great promise. Her greatest asset will eventually lie in her keen attention to technical variability and her ear for the cadences of the spoken word and its power to convey human experiences. As a symbolist, the social relevance of her play is derivable from the great power of allegory.

For Tess Onwueme, then, it is, in the words of Achebe, morning yet on creation day!

Notes

Page references to the texts are to the following editions:

1. *The Broken Calabash* (Owerri: Totan Publishers, 1984).
2. *The Desert Encroaches* (Owerri: Heins Nig. Publishers, 1985).

Tess Onwueme

Born on 8 September, 1955 at Ogwashi-Uku, Bendel State. Had her Secondary Education at Mary Mount College, Agbor, from 1968–1972. Holds a B.A. degree in Education/English, 1979, and a Masters degree in Literature, all from the University of Ife. Married with children to Prof. I.C. Onwueme. She currently lectures at the Federal University of Technology, Owerri, Nigeria.

Publications

The Children's Way, Owerri: Totan, 1982
Let's Play Together, Owerri: Totan, 1982
A Hen Too Soon, Owerri: Heins Nigeria Publishers, 1983
The Broken Calabash, Owerri: Totan, 1984
The Desert Encroaches, (An Opera) Owerri: Totan, 1985

Reviews

The Broken Calabash, Reviewed in *Time International,* 3 December, 1984 by Sunday Edem
The Broken Calabash, Reviewed in *Concord Weekly* No. 16 16–23 November, 1984.
The Broken Calabash — "another vibrant drama from a writer too soon". Reviewed in *Sunday Statesman,* 7 October, 1984 by Grace Ofunne
Tess Onwueme's *Broken Clabash* for Silver Jubilee. Interviewed by Nasamu Jacobson in *Nigerian Observer,* 24 August, 1985
The Desert Encroaches. Reviewed in *The Guardian,* 3 July, 1985 by Jane Bryce
The Desert Encroaches. Reviewed in *Sunday Concord,* 23 June, 1985 by Steve Daniel
"A writer too soon" (A critical review of Tess Onwueme's *A Hen Too Soon).* In *Nigeria Magazine* No. 151, 1984 pp. 93–95
"Cross of Two Cultures: *A Hen Too Soon"* Reviewed in *Concord Weekly* 15 April, 1985 by Jacob Aguomba.

A Hen Too Soon, Reviewed in *Nigerian Statesman,* 5 February, 1985 by Al-Bishak

A Hen Too Soon, Reviewed in *Times International,* 20 May 1985 by Jacob Aguomba

A Hen Too Soon, Reviewed in *Sunday Statesman,* 29 April, 1984 p. 4 by G.N. Echebima.

Chapter 7

Zulu Sofola's Theatre*
Olu Obafemi

Zulu Sofola, the first published female playwright in Nigeria,[1] is breaking into, and pulling tremendous weight in a male-dominated arena. There is a disturbing evidence of paucity of literary output by women in Nigeria. On this sparse showing of women in the literary scene generally in Nigeria, Zulu Sofola has herself proffered two reasons:

> The first is that in the past traditional set up of Nigeria, men were educated at the expense of the woman. Secondly, the women are more burdened with hundrum of daily life than men. And therefore it takes extra effort on the part of the female to write.....[2]

Zulu Sofola has managed to make this extra effort, reaching from the traditional backseat of women to steer the wheel of her creativity on to productive pastures, both on the stage and in publishing houses. Presently, she has six published plays: *The Disturbed Peace of Christmas* (1971), *Wedlock of the Gods* (1972), *King Emene* (1974), *The Wizard of Law* (1975), *The Sweet Trap* (1977), *Old Wines Are Tasty* (1981), and two unpublished ones: *Memories in the Moonlight* and *Song of a Maiden* (both plays have however been produced on stage and on television).

An indivisible inter-textuality exists between drama (as literature) and theatre (as performance). Any critical appraisal of Sofola's dramatic enterprise therefore must take off against the backdrop of this duality of intellectual exposure and accomplishment, of literary product and theatre praxis.

Sofola's plays show an uncanny propensity for the magical, the mythical, the legendary and the traditional. Generally, she counterpoises the old against the young, new ideas versus old tales. Her attitude seems to favour a preservation of the old even when this is untoward. This is clearly demonstrated in *Old Wines Are Tasty*. Akuagwu tells Okebuno who, after several years of sojourn both in Lagos and overseas, has become alienated from his people:

*A version of this article was first published by The Guardian Newspapers Ltd. in *The Guardian* Literary Supplement.

It is old wines that are tasty, not the new. You have tasted in white-man's country wines brewed only yesterday, but know our wine so that you may know what to mix with it.[3]

Most of her plays advocate a return to a past that could reasonably be regarded as decadent where magic, ritual and a certain overdose of the tyranny of age tower oppressively. In the tragic plays, the heroes usually demonstrate a kind of total insensitivity to the voices of reason around them. The characters' fates are sealed. They are there-fore unaware of the dangers around them. They shun all advice and move on inexorably towards their destruction.

In *King Emene*, Emene, a newly enthroned king has been warned not to perform the rites ushering in the peace week because of a heinous crime that has been committed in the king's palace. Emene's mother has actually killed the rightful heir to the throne in order that her son might become the king. Emene is not aware of this but instead of him, having been alerted, to investigate the matter, he accuses the elders of plotting to overthrow him. He continues with the rites but is driven off the shrine by a boa after which he commits suicide.

The same kind of stubbornness is demonstrated by Okebuno in *Old Wines Are Tasty*. Okebuno is an educated young man who is widely travelled. When elections approach however, he returns to his village to canvass for votes but because of his long years of separation from home, he finds himself out of place among his people. Rather than try to understand them and possibly use the influence of his uncle, Akwagwu, to win his people's support, he decides to handle the matter his own way. Okebuno is impatient. His people's strict ad-herence to tradition appears awkward to him and he would not con-done it. He insults the elders of Izuani town council. His uncle's words of admonition are disregarded while his mother's desperate plea also falls on deaf ears. He persists in taking every available wrong step until he ultimately discovers his actual status as an illegitimate child. Frustrated, he decides to return to Lagos, his base, whereupon he has an accident and dies.

A lethal magical dose similar to that of Emene, is employed in *Wedlock of the Gods*. Uloko and Ogwoma, the radical couple, al-though genuinely in love, cannot marry because Uloko cannot afford the bride price. And, since Ogwoma's parents need the money at the time to cure her sick brother, she is married to Adigwu, a higher bidder much against her wish. Shortly after the marriage, Adigwu dies and the lovers get together not waiting for the traditionally prescribed mourning period to lapse. Thereupon, the mother-in-law gets enraged. In order to enable tradition to run its course and also to avenge the death of her son whom she believes is killed by the lovers in order that they might have their way, she uses her magical prowess to destroy Ogwoma. Uloko also later commits suicide after having avenged Ogwoma's death by killing Odibei. This looks dangerously reactionary. At best, a bourgeois romanticisation with the past, the feudal past. Even if a mythopoetic vision is intended, it has not been achieved in the way in which the same can be said to emerge in the dramatic work of, say, Soyinka and Clark in plays where they share similar mythic pre-occupation.

We encounter in Sofola's plays, a *simple and even simplistic* plot all geared towards a thesis or advocating submission to the whims and caprices of age-old demigods or "custodians" of bogus tradition, for those who kick, there is no restitution. There is no redemption from the tragic consequences of dissent. Neither Emene nor Okebuno has any respite till they die. It is clear from *Wedlock of the Gods* that the playwright herself believes that it is unjust to snatch Ogwoma from Uloko simply because he cannot afford the bride-price. When Ogoli cries of shame after it has been discovered that his son has impregnated Ogwoma while still in her period of mourning, Uloko queries her:

> It was in your presence that Ogwoma was forced from my hands and given away to Adigwu. Did you speak for me? Did you let Ibekwu know that an *injustice was being done to you by his action?* Did you let anyone know that, for money, the wife, whom you had planned for your son was being forced from your hands and being given to someone else (my emphasis)[4]

Fine and courageous words! But in spite of this, Sofola still believes that they must die. Going against the tradition is a prime crime for which one must pay the supreme penalty.

Even in her non-tragic plays, Sofola is always unequivocal about her defence of tradition. *The Sweet Trap,* a fairly comic play, for example, celebrates the traditionally held supremacy of the male especially over his wife or collection of wives. In a demonstration of brute force and male chauvinism, Femi Sotubo refuses to allow Clara, his wife, to celebrate her birthday. The docile, submissive, good housewife Clara agrees initially. But a friend, whose own matrimony has previously collapsed (someone to be shunned obviously) advises Clara to hold the party at another venue. The party is eventually disrupted and, for resolution, Clara takes the advice of Dr Jinadu, her elderly uncle, and apologises to her husband with her knees firmly on the ground. This clearly shows the playwright's uncritical acceptance of certain aspects of tradition. Clara is brought cringing on her knees for trying to defend her right. Her husband is right even when he is being stupid.

Elements of myth, magic and ritual are heavily spawned and espoused in Sofola's plays. *The Sweet Trap* is deliberately set in the period when Oke-Badan, an age-old all-male festival, is being celebrated. The playwright even tries to justify its continued celebration in the play:

> It is interesting, isn't it, that our forefathers understood the value of psychological and emotional release of tensions. Oke-Badan is the epitome of their understanding of human psyche.[5]

And as a way of explaining the reason why the festival is a one-sided attack on the female sex, Sofola has this to say:

"Well, that was how our forebears felt and so it was".[6] To Sofola, all our forebears did was right and must continue. All the socio-cultural changes that have taken place since their time do not seem to matter. With colonial invasion, as we know, came western education and its attendant iconoclasticism. People began to question the pre-existing orders and those who imbibed western education uncritically even deny the most dynamic aspects of their tradition. One can however question, with some legitimacy, why a woman should be subjected to the whims and caprices of the man. Why should she be made to play a second fiddle in the society when she is also capable of intelligence and remarkable ability to contend with contemporary problems. Ogwoma is rejected by the society for daring to choose the man she wishes to marry. Even Okebuno's misbehaviour is believed to be caused by the fact that he is brought up on his mother's side. Ogbelani, a member of the council of elders states this unequivocally:

> Akwagwu should have let his (Okebuno's) father's people handle him. He is only his mother's brother and as long as Olona is still Olona, women will still be women. I am sure that had his father's people trained him, he would have known and done what every man is supposed to do.[7]

This opinion is, to say the least, regrettable, especially coming as it does from a creator with Sofola's intellectual and social exposure.

Perhaps Sofola's Christian background, coupled with her already demonstrated uncritical acceptance of tradition which she must have imbibed from her Igbo/Edo origins, is a major influence in the generation and sustenance of conflict in her plays. This is probably also responsible for her recourse to magic, myth, ritual and religious dogmatism in finding solutions to these conflicts. In *Song of a Maiden*, for instance, the union of "town and gown" which is the theme of the play is realised through a ritual wedding. A group of academics has been sent to Shao village by government for a research. The simple villagers consult their river goddess who, although welcomes the "book people",, stipulates a term for communal interaction. Professor Oduyinka, the coordinator of the project and the epitome of the "usual academic eccentricity", has to engage in ritual wedding with one of the maidens in the village. Both Yetunde, the chosen maiden, and Professor Oduyinka protest the marriage initially but they are in the end joined together. This same stereotypical theme of marriages is what we encounter in *Memories in The Moonlight*. Here, however, it is Otakpo, an elderly man of eighty that is being forced on a young girl of sixteen who already has an equally young lover. Abiona (for that is the girl's name) protests strongly against the marriage and has to leave home when it seems her parents would not listen. Surprisingly however, Abiona marries her dream man, Ugo, in the end. Perhaps the two plays' bare-bone plot and thin thematic fibre are not as disappointing as their unconvincing resolution.

As has been said, both Professor Oduyinka and Yetunde protest vigorously against the ritual wedding in *Song of a Maiden* but the two people are eventually joined together in marriage without bothering to show the audience how the two later agree to the wedding. Similarly, in *Memories in the Moonlight,* the elderly parents of Abiona insist that she marries the elderly Otakpo. How they later reconcile themselves to a situation which is contrary to their wish is a question left unanswered in the realm of metaphysics that dominates the script. It is this empirical treatment of theme and plot, coupled with an inexcusable disregard to plausibility that evinces Zulu's tendency towards the over-bled art-for-art sake dramatic tradition. *The Wizard of Law*, an adaptation of a 15th century French farcical play *Pierre Patelin* is another pointer to this fact.

In the play, lawyer Ramoni Alao, because of his nagging wife, decides to go to the market to get special clothes for "Ileya" without a kobo in his pocket. At the market, he succeeds in tricking a cloth-seller into giving him lace-material worth one hundred and eighty naira.

When later the cloth-seller arrives at Ramoni's house to collect his money as promised, the lawyer pretends to have gone mad and with the active collaboration of his wife, Rafiu, the cloth-seller is conned. When again the two meet in court in a case of goat-theft which Ramoni is defending, Rafiu is too confused to make a coherent statement. The judge thinks him mad, and together with Akpan, the accused, he is asked to go for a mental check-up.

Creative writing and literary criticism go hand in hand. For a writer to grow, he or she needs the critic to bring into light not only the merits but also the weaknesses of the work especially where such faults stand glaring and inimical to the quality of the work. The critic also has the duty, where a writer fails to do so, to remind the latter of the need to treat urgent contemporaneous issues. It is through such criticism that an author gets into limelight, and also translates nascent potential into creative fullness and maturity. There is a certain general paucity of critical work on Sofola. This is probably due to the facts that have been discussed above — the simple, monolithic plots, the negative and ineffectual employment of elements of myth, magic and ritual, and the often impossible and implausible conflict-resolution which characterises most of her works.

It is high time Zulu Sofola used the position of influence and pre-eminence she enjoys, as a leading female dramatist in Nigeria, to positive and pertinent ends. She must move away from the old school and depict realities of today. Rather than advocate the continued subjugation of the female folk in particular and humanity in general to old, out-dated lore and burdens, she should strive towards the emancipation of her sex, in particular, and the liberation of humanity in general, from enslaving codes, icons and ideas. Sofola is simple, clear and lucid as far as linguistic expression is concerned. It should be good to see her employ these qualities to serve 'noble' causes in the dramatic arts. With this consciousness of the necessity of art to be imbued with, shaped and guided by, determinate social forces of our contemporary experience, the opportunities are boundless in the arts for artists of her stature.

REFERENCES

1. We modify our claim in *The Guardian*, Saturday 16 July, 1985 that Zulu Sofola is the only published Nigerian Playwright to date. Tess A. Onwueme has published three plays since 1983.
2. *Times International*, Vol 7 No. 16, 20 January 1986
3. *Old Wines Are Tasty* **Ibadan, UPL, 1981 (page 44)** ·
4. *Wedlock of the Cods*, Ibadan, OUP, 1972 (page 43)
5. *The Sweet Trap*, Ibadan, UPL, 1977 (page 43)
6. *Ibid.*, (page 4)
7. *Old Wines Are Tasty*, Ibadan, UPL, 1977 (page 32).

ZULU SOFOLA

Of Bendel Ibo origin, she was born 22 June, 1935. Obtained her BA (English) from Virginia Union University, Richmond, Virginia, USA in 1960; MA Drama (Playwriting and Production) from the Catholic University of America, Washington DC (USA) in 1966 and a Ph.D in Theatre Arts (Tragic Theory) from the University of Ibadan. Member, Association of Nigerian Theatre Artists; Association of Nigerian Authors. Married with children to Professor J.A. Sofola. She is currently the acting Head of Department of Performing Arts, University of Ilorin, Nigeria.

Publications

Wedlock of the Gods, London: Evans, 1973
King Emene, Ibadan; Heinemann, 1975.
The Sweet Trap, Ibadan: University Press Limited, 1977
Old Wines are Tasty, Ibadan: University Press Limited, 1981
The Disturbed Peace of Christmas, Ibadan: Daystar Press Ltd., 1968
Memories in the Moonlight, Ibadan: Evans, 1986
Song of a Maiden, Ibadan: University Press Limited, 1986
The Wizard of Law, Ibadan: Evans, 1975

Unpublished Plays

"The Love of Life"
(On the relevance of Christianity to Nigerian problems)
"The Operators"
(Performed at the Arts Theatre of the University of Ibadan in May 1979)
"Queen Omu-Ako of Oligbo"
(The Role of Female Heads in Traditional Government from Agbor to Asaba during the Nigerian Civil War.)
"Maternity Series" ·
(Commissional One-Hour Television Plays, NTA — Ibadan)

Critical Writings

"Concept of Tragedy in African Experience"
(FESTAC '77 Colloquium Paper)

"The Playwright And Theatrical Image"
Nigeria Magazine Nos. 128—129, 1979

"The Position of The Church on Womanhood and Its Implications for African Theatre Arts" in *Report of Regional Consultation on Community of Men and Women in the Church Study* (An All African Council of Churches Productions, 1981)

"A Pilgrimage to a River Goddess" *Nigeria Magazine,* Nos. 126–127, 1978.

"The Bogy of African Writer's language limitations in the Creative process: The Core of the matter" (Published by University of Calabar as proceedings from 1982 English Department Conference).

"Qu Est La Panacee?" (translation of "Whither African Theatre" in *L'auteur Dramatique et la Creation Theatrale,* International Theatre Institute Publication, I.T.I Centre, Hungary, 1979

"The Theatre In The Search for African Authenticity" in *African Theology Enroute* edited by Kofi Appia-Kubi and Sergie Torres.

Conversation with African Writer by Lee Nichols, (Voice of America)

Chapter 8

Zulu Sofola: Her Writings and their Undermeanings

Ayo Akinwale

Nwazuluoha Sofola is the first published female playwright in Nigeria. The world of her plays are always succinctly chosen, her prophetic eye and cosmic consciousness of the life of the society she is dealing with in each of her plays is handled with a clear understanding of that society.

A versatile theatre practitioner, she has written and produced several plays for the stage, radio and television. She has also distinguished herself as an excellent scholar in the field of research.

The messages in her plays are usually biting, their philosophies and aesthetics purely African. Her themes and plots reveal a master craftsmanship of the theatre.

This background has contributed immensely to the works of this playwright who was trained both in America and Nigeria. Among her published plays include *King Emene* (1975), *The Sweet Trap,* (OUP 1977), *Wedlock of the Gods* (1973), *The Wizard of Law* (1975), *Old Wines Are Tasty* (1981), and *The Disturbed Peace* (1968). *Song of a Maiden. The Operators* as well as *Memories In the Moonlight* (unpublished) are also some of her plays. Others are *Love of Life,* and *Queen Omu-Ako of Oligbo.*

In terms of dramaturgy, Sofola's writings could be divided into two categories. Plays based on the traditional society which if properly diagnosed from the position of one who wishes to see the people within a society examine their plight, their struggles, beliefs, sociological organisation and social control methods, can be seen as really relevant to contemporary society. If the past and the present are but one continuum, if the past can be used to examine the present so as to make projections into the future, then these plays serve a very relevant purpose. To the material-oriented ideologists, however, they are irrelevant. Such critics are at times, usually shallow-minded encaged in the narrowness of their ideologies. These plays also rely heavily on myth, ritual and the traditional setting, a style which makes her pre-occupation in this direction quite a unique one. Such plays include *King Emene, Wedlock of the Gods, The Sweet*

Trap, Old Wines Are Tasty and *Memories in the Moonlight.*

The second category consists of plays that tackle straightforward, modern-day problems about societies and do not make the kind of statements that we find in the earlier plays. These plays delve into the various aspects of contemporary problems with a view to exposing them. Drama as a means to an end could play this noble role. Such plays include *The Disturbed Peace of Christmas, Song of A Maiden* and *The Operators,* as well as her episodes for the NTA Ibadan maternity series which include *Lost Dreams* based on the sickle cell problem, *The Night is Dark* based on *Eclampsia And by Thy Grace* based on hypertension during pregnancy and *The Showers* based on the problem of *vesico - vaginal fitulae.*

As a result of her traditional background and a deep understanding of the traditional society coupled with her innate ability and potentials for research we see her first set of plays actually rooted in the traditional society. For instance, her first published play *King Emene* which she subtitled *The Tragedy of A Rebellion,* no doubt, is constructed purely on the Aristotelian principles of tragedy. The king must not perform the rites ushering in the Peace Week because of a heinous crime which has been committed in the palace which thus makes the palace unclean. Hence, this must be expiated to clean the palace before the king can enter into the Peace Week. However, because of the hubris in the king, he rejects this prevention, refuses the two councils of the Omu and Ndi Olinzele. He has to be put in his proper place by one Chief Odogwu who actually calls him "a small rooster . . .". But backed by another Chief Jigide, he proceeds. We see him being enmeshed in a web he himself makes, he gets to a point of recognition and reversal, but too late. He enters the shrine, and he is driven by a boa. He has to and actually commits suicide. His mother who actually committed the crime, does the same.

Here again the tragedy moves from the single individual to the whole community. This transcends and goes a step further than the Aristotelian principles. For, when a noble man, pursues a noble quest and gets destroyed in the process, in the African setting, it is not only him that suffers but the whole community. Written shortly after the Nigerian Civil War, Sofola seems to be concerned not with kicking against tradition but kicking against the voice of reason. This was quite evident in the struggle between Ojukwu and Gowon which eventually led to the Civil War. She probably saw how all the peace moves by concerned people all over were thwarted. She seems to be saying that history will always repeat itself. Of course the king in question, Obi Osemene the III, is still living. Hence, the play is a product of both history and the artist's own creative intuition.

In *Wedlock of the Gods,* the prime concern of the playwright is adultery in the traditional setting. Any critic that starts off from the love between Ogwoma and Uloko therefore misses the theme or the core of the matter.

Two basic types of adultery could be identified in traditional African societies. These are the legal and the illegal adulteries. When a man is impotent and permits his wife to have a lover but with the children born in that arrangement and affair belonging to him, the adultery here is legal. Even if a woman is sterile, marries another woman and pays her dowry, allows her to have a lover she approves of, the children born by their affair belongs to her and adultery in this case is legal. However, when a married man, has an affair with a married woman, this is an illegal adultery. The highest level of illegal adultery is incest. Hence, if Adigwu died of a swollen stomach, then it is either Ogwoma has committed adultery or Adigwu himself has committed adultery. However, since Ogwoma cannot wait for the expiration of the period of mourning before having an affair with Uloko whom she would have married but for his inability to afford the bride wealth, then Odibei, Adigwu's mother, is right to conclude that she is responsible for her son's death. Her decision and recourse to magic to avenge the death of her son, is the only method for redress and social control known to the society which the playwright handles here.

One thing is clear: even though Sofola was writing about the traditional society here, the 1979 Nigerian Society was plagued with the social ill of illegal adultery. The newspapers were so full of this and other stories of divorce due to issues related to adultery. The playwright is therefore opening our eyes to those sanctions against the same ill in the traditional setting so that if we know these, we will desist from this social ill.

Although Dapo Adelugba, in his essay: "Three Dramatists in Search of a Language" in *Theatre in Africa* (1978), says that:

> The plotting is altogether too
> simple and transparent to merit serious
> consideration in the genre of tragedy ..."

he agrees that Sofola's handling of society is superb. He praises her use of language which is highly communicative and extremely lucid.

Sofola's belief in the traditional esteem in which wives must hold their husbands is totally displayed in *The Sweet Trap.* At a point when the literate women started lording it over their husbands, thus leading to fast break-ups of marriages, these women, having been privileged to know of women liberation in America, wanted to propagate same in Nigeria, irrespective of the fact that the experience of the Black American woman is not the same as that of her Nigerian counterpart living in a predominantly black society. Rather than be a "celebration of the traditionally held supremacy of the male" as claimed in the most recent criticism of Sofola's works in *The Guardian* of Saturday 18 January 1986, by Olu Obafemi, and is reproduced in the preceding chapter, the play is saying in its undermeaning that our women should understand the culture in which we operate and should not juxtapose the canons of another culture whose tenets we all wrongly imbibe and prefer over ours. This is not saying culture should be static neither should we be retrogressive or always make dramatic turn-around to the ways of our forefathers, but if there must be synchronisation of both cultures, then this must be a healthy one. One culture should not swallow the other and the culture must be imbibed through an acculturation process that provides for sifting and differential selection.

The Operators, one of her plays that deals with purely contemporary issues, seems to diagnose the issue of armed robbery within our society. Two points of focus are visible in this play. The causes of armed robbery which include unemployment, the extended family system which imposes a spouse on one irrespective of his background, the abuse of office by highly-placed people as well as the materialistic tendencies of Nigerians and hence the desire to acquire wealth by whatever means no matter how foul.

Next is a well-laid out detective means which gradually leads to the apprehension of the robbers and a plot which unfolds in such a way that one will definitely think that the playwright really must have studied criminology to be able to track down these criminals the way she does. Also, the dual face of the Nigerian so-called "big man" or "money tycoon", with all his bought appellations like "Chief" is succinctly brought out in the play. Chief Onireke who is the owner of "Silhouette Amalgamated" (a name that suggests what kind of company this is) is a business tycoon in the day and mafia or head of an armed robbery syndicate at night. This kind of bogus living characterised the set-up in the early seventies in Lagos and indeed most urban cities in the country. Up till today, the armed robbers are still ruling our streets aided and abetted by highly-placed people.

Song of A Maiden deals with the question of the relevance of university education to the society and the lukewarm attitude bordering on utter lack of interest of the universities in offering solutions to the multifarious problems of our developing society. When the play was first commissioned by the University of Ilorin in 1977 for its first convocation, the question was a burning issue. Then, it had become the concern of the nation that an impact of the number of Nigerians with qualifications from higher institutions had not been sufficiently felt in the life of the nation. There seemed to be little relevance in totality of institutions of learning and the life of the nation, particularly when the institution maintains an aloof ivory-tower posture. Today, the question is still a burning issue. The University of Ilorin Convocation Symposium for the University's Tenth Anniversary Celebrations entitled "University in Society" discussed this subject.

The play examines this problem from the point of view of ignorance of the Nigerian society, its ethos and national aspirations, caused by the foreign orientation of our university education. The Mass Wedding Festival of *Shao* Village in Kwara State was the medium of expression. For, it is believed that unless the two worlds move closer together, they will not learn from each other sufficiently enough for the cross-fertilisation and mutual influencing needed for the academia to be relevant and make an impact on the life of the nation in the type and quality of the persons produced through the humanities and the social sciences and in the quality and availability of accessories for human use produced in the areas of physical and health science.

The question thus arises, has the presence of the University of Ilorin for the past ten years of its existence been felt in the life of the people of the city of Ilorin, if one is not to mention the State of Kwara and Nigeria as a whole? Is the quality of human life of the people any better or has it been made worse? Is there a better understanding of the ways of life of the people of Kwara in their Humanities, social organisation and economic systems, their sciences and health? Has there really been a meeting point between the *Town* and the *Gown*? Or should it continue to be *Cap* and *Gown*?

These posers are pursued in a symbolic plot which seeks to place the village of Shao within the observation tower of the academia against the learned academics sent there to carry out a research work which is aimed at improving the climatology of the people, symbolising their society.

The use of ritual-wedding between one of the professors and a maiden in the village also symbolises the kind of mutual relationships needed to exist before a meaningful union of the *Town* and the *Gown* can take place.

However, as Zulu Sofola, too, says in the programme notes of the most recent production of this play:

Has the initial reluctance of the meeting of the two worlds been turned
into a mutual acceptance and co-operation of partnership in progress?
The searchlight is on. The question continues: the self-examination
proceeds *ad infinitum*.

This play now clearly demonstrates Sofola's ability to move her
writings from one society to another with ease. She allows her creative intuition to lead her to a level of high cosmic consciousness before writing so that her works are such that deal with the problem at
hand in such a chronological order that should any part of the play
be edited or removed the play is rendered meaningless.

Needless to say that her prophetic eye ten years ago in probing
into these questions of relevance is now being vindicated. For, the
University of Ilorin has just launched an Endowment Fund for a
Scientific Resource Centre that will manufacture simple mechanical
implements to cater for the use of farmers, housewives and so on at
relatively cheap prices.

All said and done, one hopes that more Nigerian women would
follow the example of this Nigerian woman who now occupies the
position Wole Soyinka is occupying amongst his male peers so that
more female playwrights will emerge from the country.

Perhaps one would also like to say that she should use her present position as the Acting Head of Department of Performing Arts
of the University of Ilorin, to encourage her female students to take
to play-writing.

Theatre critics who do not seek the undermeanings of her writings are likely to misunderstand them. A lot of information about
this energetic playwright's background is also essential for a complete
understanding of both her plays and the harvest of words that abound
in them.

It is hoped that she will also turn out more plays in the second
category to prove or negate those critics who wrongly assert that she
is purely a traditionalist and nothing more.

III

The Poets

Female Voices in Poetry: Catherine Acholonu and Omolara Ogundipe - Leslie as Poets

Dr Obi Maduakor

It is in the area of poetry that the Nigerian female writers are still trailing languidly behind the menfolk on the literary scene. They have distinguished themselves in fiction with the work of Flora Nwapa, Buchi Emecheta, and Ifeoma Okoye; and are coming up gradually even though slowly in drama with the plays written by Zulu Sofola and Tess Onwueme. And yet, it is in poetry that the young Nigerian writer is provided with the best opportunity for developing his talent. No comparable workshop is there in fiction and drama to serve as a forum for practical apprenticeship for the aspiring novelist or playwright as has been made available to the budding poet by the editors of *Black Orpheus, The Muse, Omabe, Okike, Opon Ifa* and many other Nigerian journals devoted to creative writing. These journals are known to be partial towards contributions in poetry. They have helped Catherine Acholonu and Omolara Ogundipe-Leslie to grow as poets. These two poets have consistently endeavoured to bridge the gap between the menfolk and the women in poetry. Acholonu has brought out two books of poems; Ogundipe-Leslie's collection is still awaited but those of her poems that have appeared in journals and poetry magazines compel attention by their muscular strength and disciplined structure. Ogundipe-Leslie is a veteran scholar, critic and poet.

Acholonu is relatively a new-comer to the trade but has made rapid progress since discovering her poetic talents. In nurturing her, Owerri, the capital of Imo State, is catching up with Enugu, Onitsha, Ibadan and Lagos in the area of indigenous publishing. One of the locally-based publishing companies in that city is Totan, a young company that is giving publicity to the works of young writers. Acholonu cashed in on the generosity of the Totan enterprise. Totan has published almost simultaneously, three of her works — two books of poems: *The Spring's Last Drop* (1985) and *Nigeria in the Year 1999* (1985), and a play, *Trial of the Beautiful Ones* (1985).

These books are beautifully produced. The cover designs are attractive, the sizes make for easy portability, and the print neat. But more work needs to be done in proof-reading and/or copy-editing. On page 49 of *The Spring's Last Drop* "nurtured" is misspelt "nortured", and on page 19 of *Nigeria in the Year 1999* "repatriated" is printed "repertriated". In *Trial of the Beautiful Ones* "alter" is consistently mistaken for "altar" (see page 26 for an example). The physical outlay of the poems on the printed page is an issue that should be carefully looked into in future publications. For clarity and aesthetic expediency the title of the poem should appear in bold prints and be clearly separated from the first line of every poem. In the volume *Nigeria in the Year 1999* especially, titles occasionally read like first lines.

Acholonu is one of the new voices in poetry discovered by *Opon Ifa,* the poetry chapbook published at Ibadan and formerly edited by Femi Osofisan. The Totan edition of her poems is a welcome relief to all poetry lovers who have been following her development as a poet but have had, until now, to scout through journals and magazines to reach her. To a certain extent all her poems sum up to one supreme statement on the need to be rooted, to be anchored to tradition, to a faith or some kind of supernatural agency. The absence of anchorage she calls "cultural loss", and the consequence of cultural loss is "social death". The theme of her first verse collection is "cultural loss" and the central focus of the second is "social death". The need for rooting is so crucial to her poetic sensibility that it is one of the metaphors reflected in the dedication poems in the two volumes. Her dead father had anchored her to tradition; therefore she pays homage to him in the dedicatory notice to *The Spring's Last Drop.*

> I have planted the spirit staff
> on the hard earth
> Listen now!
> Hear the rattle of the bronze bells.
> Go on, reap your harvest
> from the great beyond![1]

The intellectual achorage is fostered by her husband as the dedication homage to *Nigeria in the Year 1999* demonstrates:

> This space is dedicated
> To your quicksilver spirit
> May it bear greater harvests.
> You planted me
> On fertile soil
> Here is part of your harvest.[2]

Her concept of tradition is broad-based: it includes a people's folk-lore or legends, their creation myths and their customs and ways of life, their taboos which include the reverence accorded to lunatics as untouchables, reverence for their gods and goddesses, the provisions for title-taking, the virtues of motherhood and the unquestioning acceptance of one's destiny such as the inevitability of death. Eke, the market goddess, proves herself to be a faithful mother in the open invitation she throws to her children on *eke* day to draw from her eternal-fountain as the source of life. Taking her cue from this goddess the poet herself fulfils her role as "mother" in ths poem "The Spring's Last Drop". She would defy all distractions, all temptations and go up the steep hill to fetch the spring's last drop for her children. The poem is an ironic commentary on the image of the mother in a modern world. In the context of the present-day Nigeria where motherhood has been desecrated by the unspeakable stratagems of drug-peddling intermediaries and contract-grabbing harpies, the poem recalls all mothers to their divine responsibility as providers:

> I Obianuju
> I shall provide my children
> with plenty
> I shall multiply this drop
> they will never taste
> of the wasting fluid
> of the sea.[3]

All the distractions mentioned in the poem represent the vices in the modern world that lead to broken homes. Unfortunately, the poem as it stands in the volume named after it steers inconclusively to an end. I have therefore used in the above passage the more settled version in the poetry magazine, *Afa*.

The poem alludes sarcastically to what the poet calls "lost virtue" in the opening lines, reminding us ironically that one of the virtues that have been lost is the virtue of motherhood. This loss is lamented in the poem properly captioned "Lost Virtue". A deceptively simple poem, it looks like an ordinary love poem but what is lamented is the emergence of the modern woman. The poem is thus an elegy on the passing away of life. It would, indeed, be regarded as a love poem and it is unique in this regard because love poems are a rare species in African poetry.

All that is great and noble in tradition is concentrated on the personality of the poet's father, Olumba, who in death joined the ancestors as god:

The fire of your love
still warms our land
your name is on every lip
the young of our land
came together and
made you a deity
the old of our land
came together
and made you
an ancestor ("Surviving'', p.27).

The poet herself is designated "priestess" to her deified father, which makes her the bearer of his "spirit staff", a task she presents herself in the poem "Surviving" as lacking the courage to carry out. How she comes to be nominated the bearer of the "spirit staff" is explained in the poem "The Message". This poem is about the divination "message" delivered to the poet's family shortly after her birth regarding the identity of a dead kinsman that has been reincarnated in her. The message as delivered by the diviner *(afa)* is that the father whose life was prematurely cut short is completing his term in the life of the daughter. This is the meaning of the word "message" in the poem, that is, to announce that the father is reincarnated in the daughter. The poem endorses also the traditional belief that the seed (speak of life) that eventually becomes human life might have experienced other forms of life before becoming human. The poem has surrealistic quality typical of the entranced utterances of a diviner.

The god of divination, *afa*, speaks several times in the book. It is *afa's* function as a god to initiate man into divine mysteries. In the poem "Afa" he speaks his role in the myth of creation. He is the agent of the supreme creator entrusted with the task of creating normal human beings. In another poem "Thus says *Afa*" he urges man to be diligent and industrious, while revealing the origin of the black race. The black peoples of the world are born from the union between mother earth and sun god:

Out of their bridal chamber
came forth a black boy
bearing in his right hand
the staff of wisdom
and in his left
the staff of justice
he is the first fruit of humanity
and from him came the black race (p.25)

The lunatics of our highways and by-ways complete this picture of life in a traditional society. The lunatic is invested with dignity. In the poem "The Lunatic" he is said to be "magnetic" and "majestic", has dined with the gods and is favoured with a secret from which the sane are excluded. He is the sacred python which must be avoided by all motorists. He has seen the unameable, has tasted the unfathomable, has heard the laughter of the sea and seen the hidden face of the nightmare. It is the lunatic's privilege as the guardian of the poet. In another poem, "From the Lunatic", a mad man, who has pitched his camp on the bank of River Njaba, condemns the world as the real lunatic, for they comprehend not the language of mystery nor the peace that passeth all understanding which the river yields unto the madman. The world needs to perceive the "unfathomable thing" down the river bed to be cured of their insanity.

In her second book of poetry, *Nigeria in the Year 1999,* Acholonu evaluates Nigeria's future by what she knows of the present. The woes of the present-day Nigeria originate from the people's indulgence in moral anarchy. The anarchy is the natural consequence of the people's disrespect for religion; but it is exacerbated by the brutalities of the civil war. Indeed, the war, as the poet claims in the poem significantly entitled "Other Forms of Slaughter", ushers Nigeria into "a lustful era of anarchic bestiality". What are "other" forms of slaughter? The most gruesome is the de-flowering of teenage virgins. And so in the "Song of Beauty" the poet sings an elegy to the death of beauty, the death of honour, the death of honesty:

Singing of beauty
this day and age
is like
dancing
to a dead tune

Singing of honesty
this day and age
is like
wearing
undersize shoes (p.49).

The sentiment is crudely trivialized by the light-hearted tone. Occasionally, Acholonu fails to match the seriousness of her theme with the proper tone. This happens at the end of the poem "Afa" in which a serious commission entrusted to *afa* (the creation of undeformed human beings) is turned into a joke:

go and make the world
as I have made thee
correct my mistakes

> but do not excel me
> or I shall cut you down
> and the dogs
> will scoop the flesh
> from your bones (p.19)

The use of the slang "scoop" weakens the force of the divine threat issued in the passage.

In spite of the trivial tone, the poem "Song of Beauty" makes a serious point: an era of anarchic bestiality has been unfolded, and every other thing goes wrong — beauty is dead, mothers eat their children and men die young (see the poem "Do you stop to ask — Why?"), and politicians grow fat on stolen loot. This is the background of the Nigeria that is bequeathed to the future. In *1999* the nation is bound to give birth to a monster child who would have learnt how to speak and cheat from the womb. The new baby brandishes a book in his hand in which is printed his recipe for survival. The book is entitled *Life Made Easy,* and the chapter headings tell the whole story:

chapter one:	how to run without walking
chapter two:	education made simple — Expo 2000
chapter three:	how to make billions without sweat — the secret of ten per cent.
chapter four:	rig yourself into life-presidency (p.54).

The point however is that Nigeria doesn't have to wait till the twenty-first century to experience these ills. They have been part of the national disease since the end of the civil war.

There are further catalogues of social woes in such poems as "To Stoneface (for the records he broke)", "The Man Died Tomorrow", and "The Rain Maker". These poems are all political satires, and the identity of the political parties and personages they satirize is obvious from their contexts, but the poems are too earnest (moralistically strident) from their being too obviously propagandist. A poem like "Nigeria in the Year 1999" is melodramatic. The monstrous events going on therein are over-dramatized (notice the poem's dramatic structure).

The poems in this volume belong properly to the theme of cultural loss rather than to social death (for this is the general theme of the poems in *Nigeria in the Year 1999*). They are "Going Home" and "The Dissidents". In these two poems frivolous youths who are shown to be disrespectful of tradition suffer the consequence of their levity. In the first poem, they are excluded from communal ceremonies for renewal, and in the second they lose their lives.

Acholonu is more comfortable as a poet in her role as the chronicler of the virtue of traditional life than as a critic of social vices. Poetry of social criticism is enhanced by understatements and ironic nuances of language and by energy of rhythm as the market poetry of Odia Ofeimun and Niyi Osundare has shown. Her poetry of social criticism has none of these strategies.

On the other hand, her poetry of traditional life has passion, for it flows from the heart and is conceived from within. It is here that her gift of song and mastery of rhythm are fully revealed. The lyric grace of this poetry reflects the influence of folk song. Indeed, a poem like "Song of Water Woman" printed in *Nigerian in the Year 1999* as "Water Woman" is a direct transcription of a folk-song. Okigbo, Pol Ndu and Okot p'Bitek have helped her to exploit the lyric possibilities of the oral tradition.

Technically, she has learnt to intensify the speed and movement of her rhythms by means of the dramatic short line; but more significantly these short lines enable her to recover the patterns of spoken speech. She has had to trim[4] down poems originally written in long drawn-out lines in order to invest them with the rhythms of spoken speech; and the total elimination of punctual devices lends her poems the appearance of modernity.

Ultimately, we have to return to the question of texture, and texture is not dependent upon length. A poem like "The Spring's Last Drop" has texture; and so does the superficially simple poem "The Lunatic" (and its companion poem "From the Lunatic") or even the apparently trivial lyric, "Substance". But a good many of the poems in Acholonu's two collections lack density. This has to be related to the poet's sense of mission: what is it that is profound which the poet wishes to communicate?

It is this sense of mission that justifies the body metaphor that Acholonu tends to develop into a poetics: "poetry flows from the poet's whole body".[5] The present stage in her development is the documentary phase, the stage in which imagination descriptively recounts experience. This will have to be replaced by the interpretive phase. The stage in which events are interpreted and reflected upon in a language that reflects also the stress of the soul.

To turn from Acholonu to Omolara Ogundipe-Leslie is to enter into a poetic temperament of a totally different order. Acholonu's poetry looks inward but Ogundipe Leslie's is ambitious. Acholonu's music comes upon her naturally but Ogundipe-Leslie's poetry labours after verbal effects and intellectual concepts so that one is tempted to classify her poetry as poetry of wit. This poetry of wit is compounded by a flirtation with Marxist radicalism which has earned for it an international perspective, for it takes the destiny of the under-privileged humanity of the world as its theme. One poem[6] is entitled "Song at the African Middle Class"; another "Africa of the Seventies". "Song at the African Middle Class" is dedicated to Agostinho Neto, the radical Angolan leader who died in 1979. "Africa of the Seventies" is dedicated to an undisclosed comrade.

In "Song at the African Middle Class", a Marxist radical recounts the on-going plan (the poem is written in the present tense) to rouse the African middle class out of its present state of inertia so that it can be sensitive to its political deprivations and then be inspired to seize political power. But the question arises (and it is a crucial one); after this era of political activism spearheaded by radicals like Agostinho Neto, Samora Machel and the whole lot of the Marxist radicals, will there be another crop of such selfless leaders on the African continent? Will the new leader, the "new egungun", dance again? Will he take up the gauntlet and continue the work initiated by his predecessors?

> and if they come again
> will they dance this time?
> will new egungun dance once more
> resplendent in rich-glassed cloths?
> will they be of their people's needs,
> rise to those needs, settle whirling rifts
>
> will they say when they come
> O my people, O my people, how to love you
> delicately?[7]

There is a note of sentimentality in that very last line, but since the sentiment is not prolonged it is not allowed to inflict much damage on the poem. In the poem "Africa of the Seventies", we are reminded that the seventies are the era for the revolutionary struggle that will liberate all Africa from the tyranny of bourgeois capitalism. The poem is addressed to a comrade who should lead the revolution in his own country now that it is clear that the leadership in that country is not only incompetent but has lost all sense of direction (the clocks are transfixed). When the revolution is achieved, the poet imagines, the "hour hands can begin to move" (that is, political and economic prospperity will be guaranteed).[8]

In the next poem "Song to Black America of the Sixties",[9] Ogundipe-Leslie crosses over to the Americas in her quest for a poetic experience that is international. During her visit to America in the sixties she had the tendency to fraternize with the black Americans because their laughter, their pride, their confidence and courage, their openness of heart and warmth of mind (and body) show them to be thorough-bred Africans. But the poet soon realised that these notions ("images") were misconceived. Those qualities of soul that distinguish Africa from the rest of the world which the black Americans possessed (their big laughter, their broad smiles, their friendly men) were merely put up for show; for the black Americans insist on the difference between them and Africans. They make distinctions between "ours" and "yours" and ask funny questions about Africa: "do you guys have buildings in afrikuh?" This attitude of snobbery is worse among the educated ones, among them who would love to severe all links with Africa. One academician presented a paper at a seminar on the topic: "Towards a future without a past", which earns the poet's contempt; for how can one plan for the future without taking cognisance of the past?

A poem with the curious title "To a 'Jane Austen' Class at Ibadan University"[10] traverses the confines of the African continent only to come back to it with illuminating questions. How were the Jane Austen folk able to afford their expensive promenades and their incessant tea-soaked evenings and yet they were not known to have been engaged in gainful employments? The answer is that their leisure was sponsored by the wealth stolen from Africa. The poem is addressed to the descendants of empire builders and slave-drivers with supposedly innocent faces, refined manners and delicate speeches.

Not that Ogundipe-Leslie is always reaching out for an international experience. She has her homely moments too, as when, in "Yoruba Love", she warns inexperienced spinsters to be wary of the guilded tongue of the sweet-talking lover, which is merely a subterfuge to cheat her of her honour:

When they smile and they smile
and then begin to say
with pain on their brows
and songs in their voice:
"the nose is a cruel organ
and the heart without bone
for were the bone not cruel,
it would smell love for you
and the heart if not boneless,
would feel my pain for you
and the throat, O, has not roots
or it would root to flower my love" —
run for shelter, friend,
fun for shelter.[11]

In addition, we hear a personal voice in the confessional reminiscences of the elegiac lyric "Those Rags . . . My Rags of Time".[12] This poem is written in a sophisticated language and a complex syntax that tend to obscure its meaning; the problem however disappears if we realise that the argument of the poem is developed in three stages. The first stage is affirmation/confirmation; the second, a questioning; and the third, a resolution. In the first stage, made up of the first two stanzas, the unpleasant fact is stated, even though in a question form, that painful emotions, thoughts and hopes well up in the mind in later years with increased vigour, assuming sometimes the proportion of a flood. In the second stage (the third stanza) the basic question is asked: how does one dispose of this heart-tremor, this flood of pain? In the third stage (stanza four) this question is answered: it is not possible to regulate the emotions of the heart. They well up on their own despite the effort of the individual to control them. Memory recalls what it will at will, and it does so violently if what is recalled is painful.

The poem shows Omolara Ogundipe-Leslie at her most metaphysical (ingenious) moment. The obvious influence is Wole Soyinka. Indeed, there is a deliberate effort to outdo Soyinka in her penchant for "learned" expressions ("musk of pain", "tremulous liquescence", "interstices of the heart") and a tortuous syntax which becomes so impacted that communication is frozen. The basic conceit (in the first stanza) established an analogy between the mind and a book. The mind is a book whose pages are made up of "old thoughts, old hopes, old things". After this initial comparison, the poet is reluctant to press the analogy further, and so the analogy is dropped to enable the poet to develop a more viable option: the conceit that establishes yet a second analogy between these old thoughts (emotions) and flood. The emotions become pain which flows in the blood and builds up to a flood.

A poem in which an admirable ingenuity is displayed (out artifice) is the poetic narrative "The Nigerian Literary Scene".[13] It is a poetic narrative because it tells us who does what on the Nigerian literary scene of the seventies both in the realm of criticism and in the area of creative writing. The achievement of the poem lies in the ease with which the story of African literature in the Nigeria of the seventies is told. Art is concealed in the poem in the manner of Pope's heroic couplet. Part 1, the introductory segment of the poem, begins as follows:

One of our wags
Once mocked:
'When a man of the people

Is no longer at ease, then
Things fall apart
And lecturers are the most adept
at hurling the arrow of God
into the river between." (p.6).

And I say:
"Weep not, child,
for petals of blood will fall
and we shall be dying in the sun
returning to the shadows
after a walk in the night
through a stone country." (p.6).

In Part II, the poet chronicles the story of African literature in our universities. Naturally, the story begins from the University of Ibadan:

Why the silences at Ibadan, you ask?
the labyrinths, the violences,
The labyrinths of non-thought,
the violences of ambition.
Where the voices
and the gods
Gerard Moore's Titans? (p.6).

The titans are Achebe, Soyinka, Okigbo, J.P. Clark who were all nurtured at Ibadan, maturing later to become the giants of African literature. Here is the picture at Ahmadu Bello University:

At Ahmadu Bello
new voices too
but critical . . .
There they continue the work of him
"who lately danced and joined the ancestors." (p.8).

The last line taken from Soyinka's dedicatory homage to his father in *Death and the King's Horseman* is a tribute to the late Kolawole Ogungbesan, an eminent critic that held the chair of literature at Ahmadu Bello University till his death in 1979.

In Parts III and IV the poet looks at the state of criticism. Literary criticism in Nigeria tends to be pitched into two opposing camps: the Leavisians who appreciate works of imaginative literature for their humanising influence; and the Marxist radicals who think that it should radically transform society. As the debate goes on informally, at any rate, the student is forgotten, and when the critic eventually returns to the work, he amuses himself with half statements that are not addressed to the students nor to the public but to himself. The poem ends with a cryptic statement that emphasizes the rift (between the critic and the student): "Ah, the rivers between" (p.10).

In the last poem to be discussed in this essay, "To a Tree in a West African Savannah Country",[14] Ogundipe-Leslie pays an ironic tribute to the African weather. The savannah tree is ostensibly the subject of the poem but what fascinates the poet more is what the sun does to the tree. The sun is, of course, one of the most significant features of the African landscape and has become unquestionably a leading element in the catalogue of items on the "myth" about Africa. The sun is the source of energy but the sun can also destroy. It has baked the people coal-black but more importantly it eats into their soul. The withered outlook of the gaunt savannah tree is a metaphor for the moral, emotional and spiritual havoc the sun can inflict on mind and body, rendering the human mind insensitive to suffering, insensitive to pain:

> O tree of the scrub
> crab-red sculpture honed by time
> open-spaced in the sun's stillness
> do you perhaps see them gaunt in oak
> nakedness, gaunt in our hearts'
> torsion as the sun eats into spaces
> at home? (p.19)

Although Omolara Ogundipe-Leslie's poetry echoes with little music, it has a compactness of texture that exposes it to multiple levels of interpretation. Her imagination is intellectualised for she allows the right of her reading to bear on her poetry. There is a studied virtuosity in the structuring of thought and a conscious endeavour to outdo Soyinka in her predilection for jammed syntax. On the other hand, poetry comes to Acholonu naturally like leaves to a tree; hers is a natural imagination, the imagination of a born singer. At her best moments, poetry tumbles out of her being with unstudied ease ringing out with a vibrant rhythm and unflagging emotion. Because of her natural voice, her natural music and her fluid style it will be easier for younger poets to use her as a model than to imitate the metaphysical techniques of Omolara Ogundipe-Leslie's poetry.

REFERENCES

1. Catherine Acholonu, *The Spring's Last Drop* (Owerri: Totan Publishers, 1985), p. 7. Subsequent page references to this volume are inserted in the text.

2. Catherine Acholonu, *Nigeria in the Year 1999* (Owerri: Totan Publishers, 1985), p.9 Subsequent page references to this volume are inserted in the text.

3. Catherine Acholonu, "The Spring's Last Drop", *Afa' Journal of Creative Writing*, No. 1 (Nov. 1982), p.8. For the end of the poem in Acholonu's first book of verse, *The Spring's Last Drop*, see p.17 of the book.

4. The Poem "The Traveller" which appears first in *Okike* (No. 18, June 1981, p. 54) is broken up into brisk short lines in the version that is featured in "The Spring's Last Drop" (pp.22—23).

5. This is a slightly modified version of Acholonu's policy statement as the editor of *Afa* in that journal's maiden issue' "A true poet is something of an ogbanje or even a lunatic. You cannot make him shut up when he wants to talk, nor can you make him talk when he wants to be silent. If you think your poetry flows from your whole being send them to us" (p.11).

6. Omolara Ogundipe-Leslie's poems discussed in this essay are available in journals as follows: "Song to Black America of the Sixties" and "Yoruba Love", *Okike*, No. 19 (Sept. 1981), 34—36. "Song at the African Middle Class", "Africa of the Seventies", "To a Tree in a West African Savannah Country", all in *Okike*, No. 22 (Sept. 1982), 15—19. and "The Nigerian Literary Scene", *Kiabara*, No. 2, vol. 3 (Harmattan 1980), 6—10.

7. "Song at the African Middle Class", *Okike*, 22 (Sept. 1982), p. 15.

8. "Africa of the Seventies", *Okike*, 22 (Sept. 1982), p. 16.

9. "Song to Black America of the Sixties", *Okike*, 19 (Sept. 1981), 34—35.

10. "To a 'Jane Austen' Class at Ibadan University", *Okike*, No. 22 (Sept. (1982), p. 17.

11. "Yoruba Love", *Okike*, No. 19 (Sept. 1981), p. 36.

12. "Those Rags. . . . My Rags of Time", *Okike*, No. 13 (Jan. 1979), pp. 9—10, and also in *Rhythms of Creation' A Decade of Okike Poetry*, ed. D.I. Nwoga (Enugu: Fourth Dimension Publishers, 1982), p.99.

13. "The Nigerian Literary Scene", *Kiabara*, No. 2, vol. 3 (Harmattan 1980), 6—10.

14. "To a Tree in a West African Savannah Country", *Okike*, No. 22 (Sept. 1982), p. 19.

INTO THE HEART OF BIAFRA

Records as a humanist, the individual and group suffering of the men and women in the Biafran side during the Nigerian civil war (1967—70). Because of its essential apolitical nature, this short play is able to give, in graphic details, the pains of deprivation in a state of siege as we watch Mona, her husband, Chume, and their children suffer the realities of war. The blind daughter, Kozuru, is raped and killed by the invading soldiers in a compelling scene. Mona herself recounts the gradual death of her other children. Meanwhile, husband and wife are separated. Mona turns to a new marriage while Chume turns to the subterfuge of behaving like a victim of shell shock. The reduction of man/woman to the basic of *mere animal* existence is what makes this play compelling.

However, the refusal of the writer to treat political issues as political makes the play liable to over-simplification of historical issues. To regard the Nigerian civil war as "a useless conflict" is to be simplistic. A war that helped to question the validity of the geographical unit called Nigeria and has contributed in the on-going argument of making Nigeria define herself in the unavoidable process of realizing nationhood cannot be called unfortunate. The civil war raises, like the ensuring political breakdowns in the coups and counter coups, the central question of the reality of Nigeria. Because this play focuses on human agony without locating it realistically in a coherent historical framework, it creates vivid theatre but fails to make a significant human statement.

Dr (Mrs) Emelia Aseme Oko

TRIAL OF THE BEAUTIFUL ONES

Brings from myth the idea of the interconnectedness of the living and the dead. Like Flora Nwapa's use of the myth of water goddess, mammy-water, beautiful women are associated with the forces of this underwater goddess. Beauty is the business of the water goddess who bestows her gift on women but with penalties of early and cyclic death. The water spirits enumerate their attributes of beauty — segmented neck like the millipede, long and slender arms like the snake, smooth faces and piercing eyes.

The association of female excessive beauty with forces of evil is made real through realising Nwamma Owu's votary as a human daughter. As Nwamma's mother battles to retain a living human daughter, she narrates the inhuman peculiarities of giftedness. Nwamma is too beautiful, too intelligent, too gifted to be entirely human. She is infact a reincarnation of *Ezewanyi-Owu*, the water goddess who took form in the mother's womb.

The human reinterpretation of myth helps to understand this other world phenomenon. In other words, giftedness is too rare in the human world. Nwamma's excess of giftedness suggests that she is too good to be a human child. The play is a struggle by man to contain godhead, a struggle to retain the superhuman attribute in human form. This struggle makes this play a very moving and compell-

ing drama especially as its heightened use of poetic language enhances the conception of the ideal in a physical world.

Dr (Mrs) Emelia Aseme Oko

CATHERINE O. ACHOLONU

Nee Olumba, born 26 October 1951 in Orlu, Imo State, Nigeria.
Attended Holy Rosary School, Orlu and Girls Secondary School,
Ihioma, Orlu (1964–1971). She holds a Masters and a Doctorate
degree (1982) in English and African Literatures, respectively, from
the University of Dusseldorf, West Germany. Founder and President,
Imo Poetry Club; Member, Imo State Committee for Arts and Cul-
ture; Society for the promotion of Igbo Language and Culture and
Literary Society of Nigeria. President, Orlu Parish Christian Women's
Association (OWO). Acholonu is a "passionate poet, playwright and
literary critic." Married to Brendan D. Acholonu, they have four
children. She is currently in the English Department, Alvan Ikoku
College of Education, Owerri, Nigeria.

PUBLICATIONS

Abu Umu Praimari (Collection of Poems for Junior Primary): Univer-
sity Publishing Company, 1985.
Children's Verses I (Poetry for Junior Primary), Ibadan: Evans, 1985.
Children's Verses II or Recite and Learn (Poetry for Senior Primary),
Owerri: Heins, 1985.
Nigeria in the Year 1999 and other Poems. Owerri: Totan, 1985.
The Spring's Last Drop and other Poems. Owerri: Totan, 1985.
Western and Indigenous Traditions in Modern Igbo Literature; a
publication of the University of Dusseldorf, West Germany.
Afa: Journal of Creative Writing — Editor, No. 1, November 1982.

UNPUBLISHED PLAYS

"Myth and Rhetoric in the Poetry of Christopher Okigbo", essays co-
authored with Chukwuma Azuonye,
"The Madman's Rags, Number Sixty-Nine
"Queen Amina's Lover",

OTHER PUBLICATIONS

"The Critic of Nigerian Literature" *The Guardian* (Lagos), 12 October, 1983.

"Feminism, Women's Lib: A blessing or curse? *Nigerian Statesman* (Owerri), 10 October 1985, p. 5.

"The Igbo Folktale as Imaginative Literature" *ANU,* No. 3, 1984.

"Linguistic Processes of Lexical Innovation in Igbo." *Journal of Anthropological Linguistics* (Indiana University) 22, No. 3, March 1980.

"Ndiichie Akwa Mythology or Folklore Origins of the Igbo UWA Ndi Igbo", ed. Chukwuma Azuonye, No. 2, 1985, *Nigeria Magazine* (forthcoming)

"The Nigerian writer and the question of commitment." *The Guardian* (Lagos), 8 February 1984.

"Ogbanje: A Motif and Theme in the Poetry of Christopher Okigbo" *African Literature Today* No. 16.

"A people's revolution" *The Guardian* (Lagos), 20 January 1986 p.9. calls on Babangida's administration to launch a crusade for nationalisms.

"Specialists." Soyinka Anniversary Publications, ed. Dapo Adelugba.

"'Special' is discriminatory" *The Guardian* (Lagos), 20 December 1985, p.13. (Worried about the special treatment being given to women in this country).

"A Touch of the Absurd: The plays of Wole Soyinka and Samuel Beckett." *African Literature Today,* No. 14. 1984. pp. 12—18.

Illah, John, "Cult of Writers and Critics: A rejoinder to Catherine Acholonu's article" *The Guardian* 4 April 1984, p.9. (Attacks Acholonu for formulating a set of rules for the writers and the critics.)

REVIEW

E.N. Emenyonu's *The Rise of the Igbo Novel,* Ibadan OUP, 1978, 400pp.
In *African Literature Today* No. 13, 1983, pp. 226—228.

OMOLARA OGUNDIPE-LESLIE

PUBLICATIONS

African woman, culture and another development, *Journal of Afri-*

can Marxists, Issues 5, Feb. 1984 pp. 77–92.
"Christopher Okigbo: The Development of a Poet". *New Horn* 1,2 (1974), 17–32 Editorial. *Horn* 4, 5a, 1962 p.15.
Mbari. *Horn* 4, 5a 1962, p.8–9. (Review of Concept at Mbari Club)
"Nigerian Writers and Political Commitments." *Ufahamu,* 5 2 (1974), 20–50.
"The Palm-wine Drinkard — an assessment". Ibadan, 1970, pp.22–26.
"Pax Americana". *Beacon* 1,8, 1982, p.49. Also in *Horn* 4, 6, 1962, p.12 (Poetry).
"The Poetry of Christopher Okigbo: Its Evolution and Significance". *Ufaham* 4, 1 (1973), 47–54. See also *West Africa,* 2 April 1973 pp. 427–429. and *Studies in Black African Literature,* 4, 3 (1973), 1–8. Ten years of Tutuola Studies. *African Perspectwes 1, 67–76;* Mathali, Felix and Ogundipe-Leslie, Omolara: "Social Contexting in the Teaching of Africcan Literature" *Okike* No. 20, December 1981, pp. 82–90.

REVIEWS

King Lear. Horn 4, 5a, 1962 p.12. (University of Ibadan Drama Production, Stage Performance Review)
Leslie reviews Wole Soyinka, *Ake: The Years of Childhood in African Literature Today,* London: Heinemann, 1984, pp. 141–148.
"A Phoenix Too Frequent; Lysistrata"*. Horn,* 4, 5a, 1962, pp. 13–14. (University of Ibadan Drama Production, State performance review.)

IV

The Children
Literature Writers

Chapter 10

Junior African Literature Series by Remi Adedeji

Willfred F. Feuser

JUNIOR AFRICAN LITERATURE SERIES I

No. 1: *The Fat Woman* (1973)

This is the first volume of the "Junior African Literature Series" in simple English intended, one would assume, for children aged 8–10. The story is a very simple one, rendered in short, crisp lines, which without being poetry, remind one of free verse. It consists of short, rhythmic units easy to recite and memorise:

> One day her friend came to her:
> She came to talk to her:
> "My friend," she said, "You are just too fat,
> You have to see a doctor" (p.2)

The problem of obesity defies solution; the woman, following her friend's advice, consults a doctor, who prescribes drugs for her. The treatment is of no avail. In fact, the woman still grows fatter. She then consults a second doctor who, more sensibly than his predecessor, prescribes a natural cure:

> "You eat too much," The doctor said,
> Eat less, and work very hard."

The new therapy works wonders and after six months the woman has grown thin and more attractive.

The English used in the text is simple and straightforward and well adapted to an eight-to-ten-year old's level of understanding. Unfortunately, in the very first line there is a serious lapse in the use of tense:

> "I know a fat woman once;
> She was very fat indeed."

This should read, of course, "I *knew* a fat woman . . ." (p.3). Similarly, on page 3, the use of the masculine personal pronoun "he" slips in erroneously instead of "She," viz "the fat woman."

No. 3: *Papa Ojo and His Family* (1973, Reprinted 1979)

This booklet presents the Ojo family, consisting of Papa and Mama Ojo and their children Tunde, a boy, and his sister Nike. The family is shown in its daily rhythm of work and leisure — for the parents — and school and play — for the children. Within the time-frame of an entire week, the rhythm, work, leisure, is repeated in the opposition of working days and weekends, thus embracing the most important aspect of family life:

> "From Monday to Friday the children go to school;
> on Saturday, they do not go to school.
> They go with Mama Ojo to the market
> To buy some things for the house . . ." (pp. 7—8)

The only errors in the text are to be found on page 3, where the caption of a picture showing brother and sister should read "Every day Tunde and Nike go to school" (instead of "everyday"), and on pages 7—8, where in the above quotation a full stop had been erroneously put at the end of line 3 (after the word "market").

No. 4: *It is Time for Stories* (1973)

These first simple stories — in the sense of folktales — in the "Junior African Literature Series" are set within the framework of the Ojo family already presented in Papa Ojo and his family. Tunde and Nike help their father with his farm-work and are rewarded after the day's toil by a story-telling session. The father functions as the narrator.
   In the first story, which is well-illustrated with lively pictures, the dog and the tortoise endeavour to obtain food during a famine. The dog leads the way to steal yams from Ajayi, the farmer, but while he carries a modest quantity to satisfy his needs, the greedy tortoise takes so many yams that he can hardly move and so gets caught. The dog feigns innocence, while the tortoise is sent to prison. The narrator then imposes his own moral on the story:

> "What a clever dog!" said Tunde.
> "Yes," replied Father, "but we must not
> act like the dog. We must not steal
> other people's things. And we must not
> tell lies" (p.8).

In the three other stories told in the course of two evenings, the moral is implied rather than explicit. The figure of the tortoise, which always appeals to children, appears in three out of the four stories told in this volume.

No. 5: *Four Stories about the Tortoise* (1973, Reprinted 1979)

Here, the pattern of the framework story is abandoned. There is no more built-in-story-teller in the person of Papa Ojo, as in the previous volume, but the stories are told directly in the conventional style, beginning with the formulaic utterance "Once upon a time, there was a tortoise" (p.1). The tortoise appears with the elephant in the second story, proving his superiority over brute power. He comes to terms with the fact that the wisdom does not, and cannot, belong to any one individual in the third story, entitled "The Tortoise and the Gourd of Wisdom". The philosophical content of this story and the etiological aspect of the two remaining stories (WHY? – stories), viz No. 1, "Why the tortoise has no hair on his head," and No. 4. "Why the tortoise's back is crooked" clearly show that a higher level of understanding is being aimed at in No. 5 of the "Junior African Literature Series" than in the preceding numbers.

JUNIOR AFRICAN LITERATURE SERIES II

No. 1: *Tunde's First Day at School*

This set of the "Junior African Literature Series" is of a slightly larger format than the set previously reviewed. It would seem to be intended for children in the 10–12 age bracket. Unfortunately, the Readers are not numbered but one might surmise, on the basis of the thematic progression, that the readers could be numbered 1–3, as has been done herein.

Quite obviously, the child's most momentous encounter with his unfolding social world is his first day at school. The story starts with a brief review of his pre-school activities. More complicated tenses than in the previous series, such as the pluperfect, are freely used:

> "Tunde was six years old when he started to
> go to school. Before that time he had stayed at
> home while his older brothers and sisters went
> to school. He could not go with them then
> because he was not yet six years old" (p.1).

The fears, hesitations and joys of the first day at school, which is also a day of self-discovery, are meticulously depicted. The child learns to define his identity, even though it might first be formulated for him by proxy:

"Is there anything I can do for you?" The headmaster asked Tunde's mother.

"Yes, Sir," she replied. "This is my son. His name is Tunde Ojo. He is six years old and so I have brought him to school." (p.9)

The little beginner is bewildered during his first arithmetic lesson, but he soon finds his feet:

"But when it was time for story-telling, he looked more cheerful. Tunde likes stories" (p. 13). Overall this is a good, realistic and lively description of a momentous event in any child's life.

No. 2: *Tunde's Birthday Party* (1983)

Another important event in a child's life — and an event increasingly celebrated by the children of the westernised Nigerian elite, especially in an urban culture — is his or her birthday. In Tunde's case it takes place not too long after his first day of school, when, as we might recall, he was six years old, for he is now turning seven.

The birthday celebration allows the child to play a central role in the house, albeit for a very short period. The children get together on a voluntary basis of elective affinities, out of friendship, and not on the basis of societal coercion, as in the case of school attendance. On this occasion the child chooses his own friends. As Tunde tells his mother when she goes to market:

"And don't forget to buy some drinks too,"
her son added. "For I shall invite all my
friends to my party. I shall invite Femi and
Dotun and Tayo. I shall also invite all the
small children who live in our compound. And
we shall have a nice time together" (p. 5).

What strikes us in this passage is the list of names: Femi, Dotun, Tayo. The text is clearly ethnically determined since all the children belong to a single ethnic group, the Yoruba. Although the choice of names can be defended on grounds of realism because the population in non-urban communities, especially in the three Western States, tends to be ethnically homogeneous, it curtails the usefulness of the book, and of the series in general, somewhat in the wider context of the Nigerian society, especially in the non-Yoruba-speaking areas.

No. 3: *Tunde Visits Ibadan* (1983)

Here, the horizon of the child is gradually extended from the village community where the Ojo family is at home, to one of the big urban centres, namely Ibadan. We must bear in mind that Tunde's father is a farmer, while his mother is a trader. Tunde's uncle, who comes home to his village from Ibadan to spend the Christmas holidays, takes the boy with him in his motor-car: a hint at the success of the social climber in the urban environment. To the child, Ibadan is the "Open Sesame" to a new and unknown world, a world with such fascinating features as television:

"What's a television?" Tunde asked (p. 21).

The topography of Ibadan in the book is painstakingly realistic, and one easily recognises its landmarks like the Cocoa House and the University, and the quarters of the city like Agodi, Gbagi, Dugbe and Sango.

Remi Adedeji: *Stories My Mother Told Me*

This is a collection of folktales adapted for school children ranging from the age of ten to the age of thirteen. It contains a total of nine stories, three of which are of the WHY — story variety, viz —

"How the Leopard got his spots,"

"Why Cats eat twice," and

"Why the Tortoise's neck is short."

The book is well-illustrated in black and white by a gifted graphic artist, M.O. Onimole.

To each story is attached an appendix of two to three sections designed to ascertain the reading comprehension of the pupils, proceeding from the simple to the complex. The following sections of exercises appear in the book:

"How much do you remember?"

"Give the opposites of the following words used in the passage."

"Now, tell the same story by filling the gaps."

"Can you tell the same story by completing the following sentences?"

"Tell the same story by arranging the following sentences in the right sequence"

"Choose suitable words to complete these sentences about the story.

"Which of these sentences is true or false according to the story."
Overall, this is a good collection with well-graded and variegated comprehension exercises.

REMI ADEDEJI

Born in April 1937 in Okemesi — Ekiti in Ondo State. Attended St. Michael's School, Okemesi—Ekiti and the Methodist Girls School, Ilesha, 1943—50. Had her secondary education at St. Anne's School, Ibadan, 1951—1955 and obtained the West African School Certificate(Grade 1) 1955. Did her post secondary education at the Nigerian College of Arts, Science and Technology, Ibadan, 1956—1958 where she obtained Advanced Level G.C.E. in 1958; University College, Ibadan, 1958—1961 and obtained the B.A. (London) degree in 1961. Obtained a post-graduate diploma in education at the University of Ibadan, 1968 and a master's degree from the University of Ife, 1978. Has 23 years of postgraduate teaching experience, 19 of which are in post-secondary institutions. Vice-President of the Nigerian English Studies Association. Member of the following organisations: Educational Studies Association of Nigeria; Reading Association of Nigeria; Health Management Committee, Ijero District, Ondo State 1978—79; National Section of the International Board on Books for Young People (IBBY). Member, Oyo State Branch of the National Readership Promotion Campaign Committee. Board of Governors of different Schools at one time or the other. Associate Editor for Nigeria for *Book Bird.* Currently Acting Head of Department, Languages and General Studies (Later Liberal Arts), The Polytechnic, Ibadan from 1979 to date. Married with six children.

PUBLICATIONS

The Fat Woman. Ibadan: Onibonoje, 1973.
Papa Ojo and his family. Ibadan: Onibonoje, 1973.
It is Time for Stories. Ibadan: Onibonoje, 1973.
Four Stories about the Tortoise. Ibadan: Onibonoje, 1973.
Stories My Mother Told Me. Ibadan: Heinemann, 1978.
Tunde's Birthday Party. Ibadan: Onibonoje, 1983.
Tunde Visits Ibadan. Ibadan: Onibonoje, 1983.
Tunde's First Day at School. Ibadan: Onibonoje, 1983.
Moonlight stories: How the tortoise married the king's daughter and

Other Stories. Ikeja: John West, 1986.
Code-Switching Among Yoruba-English Bilinguals (forthcoming)

OTHER PUBLICATIONS

"The Advantages of Reading", *Nigerbilios* Vol. 8(4) Oct. 1983.
"English and Communication for Business and Secretarial Studies" *POLYCOM* Vol. 1
"Oral Presentation and Teaching of Grammatical Structures in English", *Teachers' Forum* Vol. 7, No. 1 1979.
"Problems of Writing and Publishing for Children in Nigerian Languages, *Nigerbiblios* Vol. 9 (1) Jan, 1984.
"The Teaching of spoken English in our Schools' *(Tutors' Journal,* Vol. 1, No. 2 January/April 1971).
"Writing for Children" *Bendel Library Journal,* Vol. 2, No. 2, December 1979.
"What my country does for the gifted child".

UNPUBLISHED WORKS

"Developing Reading Habits in Children" — a paper read at the Symposium on 'Meeting the Cognitive and Affective Needs of Today's Children."
"Guidelines for Writing for Children" — a paper read at the Federal Ministry of Education Workshop on Development in Supplementary Readers in Nigerian Languages.
"Illustration and self-image: Social and Artistic Responsibilities" — a paper read at Unesco/U.I.A.R.M.C. Conference and Workshop on African Languages — Horizon 2000: Folklore as Source Material for Children's Books.
"The Performance of an Infant School Child" — a paper read at the Conference of the 1st Nigerian Psychological Society.
"The Role of Mother as Teacher of Pre-School Child" — a paper read at the Institute of Education University of Ibadan, Conference on Women and Education in Nigeria.
"Toys for Learning" — a paper presented at the Delta Steel Company, Aladja, Warri — Workshop for the D.S.C. School Teachers 24–28, October 1983.
"Understanding the Child" — a Paper presented at the Delta Steel Company Aldja, Warri — Workshop for the D.S.C. School Teachers, 24–28 October, 1983.

CHRISTIE A. AJAYI

Born 13, March 1930 in Ile-Oluji, Ondo State. Was educated at Kudeti Girls' School (now St. Anne's School) Ibadan, and later at the United Missionary College, Ibadan where she was trained as a Grade II teacher in 1951. Obtained G.C.E. O' Level in 1954; a Diploma in Child Development in 1958 from the University of London's Institute of Education. In 1971, she obtained a Diploma in Elementary School Administration Leadership from San Jose State University, California, U.S.A. Between 1952 and 1978, she had teaching experience in various educational institutions including the Anglican Girls' Schools, Ondo and orita Mefa, Ibadan, respectively. West London Primary School; Staff School, University of Ibadan; Maryhill Convent School, Iwo Road, Ibadan and the University of Lagos, Faculty of Education. She also acquired a wealth of administrative experience on her various posts. Member, Board of Governors, University of Lagos 1972–1978 and St. Mary's Girls School, Ikole – Ekiti, Ondo State, 1976–1980. She belongs to numerous societies including University of Ibadan Women's Society; Ladies Dining Club; University of Ibadan Red Cross Group; International Women's Society; Association of Nursery Schools, Lagos; International Board on Books for Youth (IBBY); World Organisation of Early Childhood Education; Committee for African Illustrators Exhibition for Bologna Book Fair. Presently residing at 8 Macauley Road, University of Ibadan. She is married with five children.

PUBLICATIONS

Ade, Our Naughty Little Brother. Ibadan: Onibonoje, 1974.
The Old Story Teller. Ibadan: Onibonoje, 1975.
Akin Goes to School. Ibadan' AUP. 1978. (Co-authored with M. Crowder) (Has a Yoruba translation by C.A. Ajayi).
Alli's Bicycle. Ibadan: Macmillan, 1982. (The Parrot Series)
Emeka and his Dog. Ibadan: Macmillan, 1982. (The Parrot Series).
My Book of Animal Riddles. Ibadan: Macmillan, 1982.
(The Parrot Series).
Tinu's Doll. Ibadan: Macmillan, 1982. (The Parrot Series);

The last three elementary readers are for children aged between 6–7 years. They are not numbered but have been arranged, according to their ISBN, in the following sequence' *Alli's Bicycle* (1982), *Tinu's Doll* (1982). *Emeka's Dog* (1982). They are simple, clear, well-illustrated and show a truly national character, with Nigeria's three major ethnic groups — Hausa, Yoruba, and Igbo — being represented in the figures of Ali, Tinu and Emeka.

Each volume consists of 12 whole-page multi-coloured pictures captioned in each case by a single-line sentence, e.g., "This is Ali's bicycle," or "This is Tinu's Doll."

UNPUBLISHED

"Books for Children — What to Write and How to Write."
Presented at the Writers' Workshop, Benin.
"The English Language Teacher and the Technical Student" (Paper presented at the Conference on English Language Studies in Higher Institutions at Bayero University, Kano.

Chapter 11

Audrey Ajose in Children's Fiction
Obiageli C. Nwodo

Yomi's Adventures is Audrey Ajose's first book and it delves into the realms of adventures for children. In this story the author takes us on an excursion not only into Ibadan, one of the largest and oldest cities in Nigeria, but also into the city of London depicting its architectural magnificence and splendour.

The story is built around a teenage girl, Yomi Kayode, whose love for photography prompted her father to buy her a camera. Armed with the latter and a timely photographic competition advertisement by a firm (Crispies and Company), Yomi competes and comes out successful. She wins a prize — an-all-expense paid trip to London. She sees in this journey, a beautiful prospect but could have hardly foreseen the package of unpleasant but thrilling adventures that await her.

The journey proceeds from Lagos to Kano Airport from where Yomi receives a present from the Kano representative of Crispies and Company. The Black Plastic Zipper bag received in all innocence is assumed to have contained choice selection of Crispies products. However, as the story unravels, we discover that the bag contains much more than chocolates and biscuits. Very little did Yomi know that she has been used by safe-breaking syndicates with international connection. This time, stolen diamonds from South Africa en route to London were lodged into the "harmless looking sweets" offered Yomi as a present by the supposedly Kano representative of Crispies, knowing fully well that the Customs will not expect an innocent girl like Yomi to be carrying such gems. Luck ran out on them however, but only after Yomi's excursion has been interrupted by some nasty experiences.

In general, the theme of this story is embedded in the traditional Christian morality that the good will triumph over the evil. In developing the plot, the story links up three countries, namely: South Africa, Nigeria and Britain. The plot development however, differs from country to country. In Nigeria, the early part of the heroine's life and the early part of the plot development correspond and could be called the age of innocence, with limited chances of anything good or evil. In the first chapter, for instance, Yomi is seen engaged in routine house work with the mother. She interacts amicably with her friends. Pa Olu is seen bowing out after an unsuccessful business venture, in photography, which is marred partly by his uncontrolled drinking habits. For Yomi's love of photography, her father promises her a camera. Armed with the latter she wins a competition that gives her a chance not only to travel to Britain but also exposes her to crime and evil. Mr. Percy, an unconfirmed criminal succeeds in setting up a trap for Mr. Williams in a bid to prove him incompetent and take-over his job. Jack, the fair-headed man of the big diamond robbery in South Africa, working in close collaboration with Mr. Percy, succeeds in carrying across his loots to London with Yomi as the innocent trafficker. Despite the apparent successes of these criminals and the initial setbacks for Mr. Williams, he is vindicated at the end living out the truism: 'there is no Easter Sunday without a Good Friday'.

In all, what really fascinates one is the plot and the craftsmanship of the novelist. She succeeds in choosing appropriate circumstances to give accurate and exquisite expression to her ideas. The dog digging circumstances come to mind here. One cannot but marvel at the poetic relationship between the word "Dig" which informally translates "to like" and "to start eating", and the dog actually digging the earth for Crispies. It is this combination of the poetic and the actual in the photograph that really won the prize for the photographer — Yomi. But the real winner of the prize is the novelist herself who uses the imaginative lens of her craft to put it all together so graphically.

Yomi's Adventure is clear, concise and an enjoyable leisure reading for the pre-teens as well as early teens. It is as educative as it is fascinating and the reward for honesty and courage translates a trip to London and Paris for a Nigerian girl with a Camera.

AUDREY AJOSE

Publications

Yomi's Adventures: London and New York: C.U.P., 1964.
Yomi in Paris: London and New York: C.U.P., 1966.

ANNE AKPABOT

Publications

Aduke makes her Choice. Walton-on-Thames: Nelson, 1966
Sade and her Friends. Walton-on-Thames: Nelson, 1967.

Reviews

Aduke makes her Choice. Reviewed in Education, 2, 3/4, 1969, p.40
Reviewer: S. O. Ehigiato.

ROSE ANIZOBA

Publication

The Adventures of Mbugwe the Frog. London and Ibadan: OUP, 1965 (The Little Bookshelf Series)

The Writings of Teresa Meniru

Charles E. Nnolim

Teresa Meniru has remained, from beginning to end, a writer of children's books. With Flora Nwapa, Ifeoma Okoye, and a new writer on the scene, Charry Onwu, she is among the group of Nigerian women who are devoted to promoting and encouraging literary awareness in Nigerian children and adolescents. Her works, chronologically, are as follows:

The Carver and The Leopard, 1971
The Bad Fairy and the Caterpillar, 1971;
The Melting Girl and Other Stories, 1971;
Unoma, 1976;
Unoma at College, 1981;
The Drums of Joy, 1981;
Footsteps in the Dark, 1982.

Although the books get progressively longer, from *The Carver and the Leopard* (20 pages) to *Unoma* (58 pages), to *Unoma at College* (76 pages), to *Drums of Joy* (91 pages), to *Footsteps in the Dark* (97 pages), the audience (children and adolescents) remains the same. There is a shift in the subject-matter beginning from *Unoma* in 1976. Before *Unoma,* all the stories were folk and fairy tales already well known in Igboland. From *Unoma* onwards, she makes an attempt at originality and invents her own stories aimed at highlighting the adventures of her heroes and heroines who are naturally good within but get into all sorts of scrapes and adventures because of their bold-headed and irrepressible natures. In spite of the shift in subject-matter already noted, the themes and the method remain frozen from beginning to the end, as will be discussed later. Teresa Meniru, the spiller of children's yarns started her writing career (which has now spanned two decades) with a manifesto in *The Melting Girl and other Stories:*

Nowadays, we are becoming too dependent on mechanical gadgets for our entertainment, and we often feel lost without them. But in our parents' days, things were very different. Our mothers used to entertain the family, and often told stories or sang songs. Some of the stories had songs in them and the children would join in the chorus.

My mother had a large stock of such songs and stories, and there is, nowadays, the danger of such things being lost. I have therefore tried to preserve many of them in writing. . . . I hope others will feel inspired to preserve in the same way Ibo folklore from their childhood days.

So, most of the tales are already well-known folk and fairy tales with which anyone who grew up in the village would be familiar. Re-telling a stock of stories already in existence may attract no particular attention. It is what the author does with them that is of importance. One, therefore, notices from the onset that Meniru chooses these tales in which the underdog, usually a foundling, triumphs in the end over jealousy, evil machinations, and sheer wickedness. The first story "The Melting Girl" lays emphasis on the triumph of the innocent and the maltreated over the wicked schemings of fellow people (usually jealous co-wives) in a polygamous setting. Here, a wicked King forcibly acquires the only goat owned by a poor woman (even though the King has several of his own), slaughters it, and allows the poor woman the heart, the liver, and the fat. The fairy tale subsumes the marvellous, so from these three portions three beautiful girls emerge, and the King married the girl that grew out of the fat of the goat. The King is advised not to allow her to go near the fire or cook any food or she would melt. But on the occasion of the King's absence, jealous co-wives force the new wife to do some cooking and she melts in the process, except the heart from which the fairy good-mother-in-law lets emerge a more beautiful woman whom the King happily marries again after sending away all the jealous wives. And they lived happily ever after.

The next story with the foundling tradition is entitled: "The King with no Heir" which centres around five wives of the King one of whom is hated and isolated by him.

The King's heir born of the hated woman is thrown into the river by her jealous co-wives who annouce that the new baby is a girl. But an old woman discovers the baby in the rushes, raises him, and when he grows up, returns him to the King who, on discovering the trick played on him by his favourite wives, sends them all away and takes to his heir and his mother who now reside with him in the palace.

The story of the underdog continues in Meniru's second collection, *The Carver and the Leopard*. The folktale "The Wife with a Tail" tells how a jealous fifth wife reveals to the King that his second wife whom he hates and starves has a monkey's tail. In the gathering ordered by the King in which the wife with the tail is to be publicly exposed, the tail which the fifth wife actually found on the second wife is mysteriously transferred to the fifth wife who is a gossip. The King is angry, sends his fifth wife away and "then took his second wife and loved her, so that she was happy again." The foundling tradition is certainly not forgotten in another collection. *The Bad Fairy and the Caterpillar* where the third story entitled "The Cruel Slave Girl" narrates how a slave girl on the death of her mistress usurps the place of the girl she was brought to nurse and impersonates her. The little girl's older sister who had all along taken and treated her as the slave discovers through a wine-tapper that the "slave" is her sister and her "sister" is actually the slave. All end happily, however; "the two sisters were so happy that they forgave the slave girl for what she had done". With this collection ends the first phase of Meniru's writing career as the next phase beginning with *Unoma* forces her to be more inventive. And with *Unoma,* the reader notices that Meniru has discovered a formula from which she seems to have found it impossible to deviate.

The formula reads like this: the protagonist who is an underdog is both bold-headed and incautious. He/she gets kidnapped at a certain point, suffers ordeals, is rescued and after a long time during which the parents give him/her up for lost, are happily reunited with the young adventurer, and all is well afterwards. The adventures and scrapes in which the protagonist is involved are sometimes unedifying, and one searches in vain for any moral or philosophical meaning or lesson attached to it all. The protagonist ends up not certainly wiser or chastened, and only the final reunion with the parents ends a life of heedless and, sometimes, thoughtless involvement in hair-raising adventures. The normal journey motif in literature of the young — from immaturity to maturity, from ignorance to experience, from naivete to sophistication, is always lacking in Meniru's stories. Neither honesty nor morality nor honour nor hardwork nor healthy cunning, is preached by Meniru: only heedless, bold, fearless, daring enterprise which in most cases land the protagonist in a mess, is emphasised. And art gives way to a series of episodic misadventures, too often crowded into an unbelievably short span of life, that the reader does not fail to wonder if any one life-time can contain such a number of hair-raising experiences.

Unoma, for example, is accused of, and exonerated from, stealing in school, gets initiated into the secret masquerade cult as a last resort to save her life, escapes from the murderous chase of a thief whom she spied, nearly drowns in the swirling waters of Azi Lake in trying to save a drowning classmate, unwittingly gets the family house on fire during a frying misadventure from which her brother is saved at the nick of time, and finally passes the entrance examination to a Teachers' College to fulfil the wishes of her father who wants all his children to be literate to compensate for his own illiteracy which made it possible for a dishonest friend to cheat him.

Unoma at College is a sequel. It records the misadventures of a teenage Unoma at a Teachers' College, predictably irrepressible who first led a crusade against their pilfering cook, is caught and gagged and tied for the kill by the cook's husband, is rescued at the eleventh hour, before she is plunged into a ravine in a bicycle accident where she barely escapes death again when a search-party rescues her from a menacing leopard. After this, she is involved in a gas-stove accident in the Technical Kitchen during a cooking session, during which she pulls out their Home Economics external examiner to safety. Surprisingly, she emerges first among her class in that accident-prone examination, goes home and single-handedly takes her father to the hospital for a successful operation at the mission hospital. Raw courage and a great presence of mind are clearly her endowments, not caution or wisdom.

From here, Meniru moves to *Drums of Joy*. The same formula repeats itself as the heroic, Nnenne Mbonu (Nene Bon) goes to fetch fodder for Ma Chinyere's goats, is kidnapped by a group of evil men, escapes and rescued by a missionary, Father Joe, and is educated in a convent manned by Sister Gertrude. In the convent where she is treated kindly as a foundling, she runs into scrapes. First, in a game of hide-and-seek with other girls, she locks herself into a cupboard without keys and is rescued again at the eleventh hour when the carpenter prized open the cupboard. Before anyone can catch his breath, she rescues a baby she is carrying from a menacing pig which bites her and lands her in a hospital. Emerging from the hospital she undertakes a trip to Kaduna with Sister Gertrude and predictably is left by the train at Kafanchan as she struggles with a thief who had snatched Sister Gertrude's watch. The train is recalled from the tracts to pick her up, and she is finally reunited with her family through the detective work of Sergeant Eddy Inyang at a ceremony in which she receives a prize "for the bravest girl" in her set.

Footsteps in the Dark completes the obverse side of Nnenne Mbonu's adventures, as Meniru tries to balance her stories by focusing on the adventures of a boy rather than a girl. Again, the same formula, with minor configurations is followed. Here, Uche Okafor, alias Uche Barrow, is farmed out by his parents, through a middle man, Josephat Okoli (greedy, rapacious) to a rich woman (Madam Cash). In the latter's house, Uche is framed by Madam Cash's spiteful nephew and accused of stealing her money. Through the intervention of the landlord, Uche is exonerated as the nephew is discovered to be the real thief. On leaving Madam Cash's house and unable to claim his earnings from Josephat Okoli, he is captured by a gang of thieves who train him as a robber in their den. Uche turns tail in a robbery operation, is impressed into service by Mr. Obi where the latter's wife accuses him of stealing meat nightly from the soup-pot. A wild cat is discovered to be the culprit and Uche is allowed to go to school where, because of his leadership abilities, he is made the class prefect. In the end, the gang discovers him and attempts to kidnap him at school. Failing in this attempt, they kidnap Mr. Obi's daughter, Ego, to force Uche to surrender himself to them, to forestall his revealing their hideout. Uche finally leads a team of policemen to the gang's den and they are captured. Ego, the little girl is rescued, Uche is wounded but recovers in a hospital. Finally, Uche is given a "full scholarship to cover all fees and expenses during his primary and secondary education." On the day of the award, he is happily united with his long separated family. Meniru is a purveyor of the happy ending in all her stories.

Intriguing, and worthy of recording, is the similarity of the endin of the *Drums of Joy* and *Footsteps in the Dark*. The *Drums of Joy* ends thus:

> Nnenne stopped, looked right as the spotlight turned right. She saw Father Joe, the kindly priest standing smiling. Beside him stood an older man and Sergeant Inyang . . . Like a veil drawn aside, light began to dawn on Nnenne. Surely she knew the older man? She knew him! She jumped up shouting, "Papa! Papa!". . . . . Nnenne found herself held in her father's arms . . .
>
> And so, Nnenne returned home. Word went before them. The drums that were to sound at her final funeral rites sounded in joy to welcome her home. Clara finished the story, wiping her eyes . . . "she (Clara) is also that Nnenne whose story she has just told you."

Here, the story-teller is the heroine herself. Now, without any significant variation, here is how *Footsteps in the Dark* also ends:

> But Mr. Obi walked towards the house. Uche hurried after him. Before they got to the door, a middle-aged man and a woman came out. They looked very familiar and Uche stopped in his tracks. He closed his eyes. Then he opened them again. The couple were still there and unless he was dreaming, they were his parents . . . Taking a jump, Uche threw his arms around them crying, "Papa! Mama!" . . .
>
> "But is this really a true story? It certainly did, my dear," replied Grandma, "for the one who told the story, your father, is none other than Uche Barrow."

In sum, the one lesson Meniru seems to teach the children in her stories is contained on the last page of *Footsteps in the Dark,* just discussed. It is contained in the following words: "So you see, my dears", said their Grandma, "both boys and girls can be brave."

If Meniru hopes to write for a more mature audience in the future, she has to understand that serious literature is like a mask: it is full of mysteries. It is like a dance: it contains intricate rhythms.

TERESA EKWUTOSI MENIRU

Nee Ajuba was born to P.I. and Adaeze Ajuba on the 7 April, 1931. Holds a Higher Elementary Certificate from Holy Rosary Teacher Training College, Ihiala. Obtained London University Institute of Education, Teacher's Certificate from Coloma College, Wickham Court, West Wickham Kent, in 1955, Principal, St. Teresa's Training College, Aboh via Enugu from January 1956 to March 1959. An educationist who taught in many schools and colleges. Later worked in both Federal and State Ministries of Education before retiring in July 1984. She is Married to Engr. G.U. Meniru and they have seven children. Presently proprietress, Little Flower of the Child Jesus Nursery/ Day Care Centre, Enugu, Nigeria.

Publications

The Bad Fairy and the Caterpillar, Ibadan; Evans, 1971.
The Carver and the Leopard, Ibadan: Evans, 1971.
The Melting Gril and other Stories. Ibadan: Evans 1971.
Unoma, Ibadan: Evans, 1976.
Omalinze, Ibadan: O.U.P., 1977, (co-authored work)
Unoma at College, Ibadan: Evans, 1981.
Footsteps in the Dark, Ibadan: Macmillan, 1982.
The Drums of Joy, Ibadan: Macmillan, 1982
Ibe the Camon Boy, Ibadan: A.U.P. (Forthcoming)
Last Card: (a novel based on Nigeria/Biafra War). Ibadan: Macmillan.
 (Forthcoming)
The Lion on the Hill. Ibadan: Macmillan. (Forthcoming)
The Mysterious Dancer. Ibadan: Macmillan. (Forthcoming)
Uzo: A fight with fate. Ibadan: Evans. (Forthcoming)

Chapter 13

The Fiction of Martina Nwakoby

Juliet Okonkwo

Martina Nwakoby's fiction is deeply rooted in Nigerian social life. She transmits, most admirably, the traditions, prejudices, ambitions, virtues and vices which are prevalent in traditional and contemporary Nigerian life. Her style is simple and the vocabulary within easy access. This simplicity is enhanced by her employment of short chapters which develop each idea or movement in her narrative within a chapter. So far, she has confined herself to the chronological unfolding of events, allowing her material to build up gradually before finally exploding in one big crescendo.

A Lucky Chance published by Macmillan in 1980 is a delightful 65 (sixty-five) page children's novelette. It tells the story of Chisa Ikenga who, at nine years old, is taken away from his native village of Omonda where he lives a poor, but happy, life as the only son and child of Dede Ikenga, his father, and Mami Ikenga, his mother. Dede Ikenga is a watch repairer who supplements his income from the trade through assorted odd jobs and farming; while Mami Ikenga combines her housewifery with petty-trading. Chisa is taken away from this secure, happy life of love and intimacy with his parents by his Uncle Kulu Ikenga, a chief clerk with a Government Ministry of Ota, who promises to bring Chisa up like his own child and send him to secondary school. Excited at the prospects of a wider horizon and a brighter future, Chisa and his parents consent to the proposal.

The reality, however, turns out to be different from the expectations, for Kulu Ikenga's wife and her children, especially the eldest son of the house, Dozie, proceed right from the start, to treat Chisa worse than a servant, for;

> Chisa was used in the house like a paid servant. In spite of his services, his cousins, Dozie and Feka, were unkind to him and that was because Chisa often earned their father's praise (p.32).

This is in marked contrast to the experience of Laye who goes to live with his uncle in Konakry in Laye's *The African Child.* Not only does Chisa have to work harder than his age merits, but he is also deprived of reasonable food, leisure, or opportunity to study. He is stopped from going to school for a term, the last term of the school year, which makes him lose an entire year. But Chisa is lucky to find a friend in Nedu, another boy who is an inmate of the block of flats where the Ikengas live. Nedu relieves Chisa's boredom and unhappiness, sharing every imaginable thing that he can share — food, books, company, and sympathy.

When Chisa is allowed to go to school, he can do so only in the afternoon. Being a very well-brought up boy, he works hard at school and so maximises every opportunity that he earns the recognition and praise of his teachers. He even makes up for lost time when he is promoted a class above his mates due to his brilliant performance in his first examinations. The test comes when, in spite of obstacles placed in his way, he sits and passes the Common Entrance Examination and is posted to Government College in Abuja, to the chagrin of Mr. Kulu Ikenga and his wife and their son, Dozie, who fails the examination for the third time. An underhand criminal plan by Kulu and his wife to make their son, Dozie, take Chisa's place in the college is foiled by the Headmaster who announces also that Chisa has won a Government Scholarship which ensures for him five years of completely free secondary school education. There is nothing anybody can do now to stop Chisa's progress. He has earned all this through hard work, and exemplary behaviour.

A Lucky Chance is structured around the "Orphan makes Good" of folklore tradition, except that its chief protagonist, Chisa Ikenga, is not really an orphan, since both his parents are alive. To all intents and purposes, however, Chisa might well be regarded as an Orphan, for at Ota where most of the action takes place, he is so far away from his parents that contact between them is non-existent, and they cannot intervene on his behalf. At Ota, his whole life and welfare depend entirely on his uncle's family whose ostensible intention of taking him away from the village of Omonda is deceptive. The real reason is revealed by his uncle's wife who states resentfully: "Life won't be too pleasant, I am afraid. He was brought here to help and I'll see that he does just that" (p. 23).

The role of Mrs Kulu Ikenga in the story accentuates its folktale quality, for she fills in the part of the wicked step-mother, whose maltreatment of her ward is mind-boggling. To the extent that she indulges her children, she intensifies her acts of cruelty and deprivation of young Chisa.

Chisa's teacher and headmaster who help to resolve the conflict in Chisa's favour, act out the parts of the spirit that always come to the rescue of the oppressed, good, and dutiful children in folktales.

But in spite of its affinity with the folktale, *A Lucky Chance* is a very realistic, story. The setting is very convincingly etched. The village of Omonda, in its quiet pastoral retreat, with mud huts and peaceful foliage, is a recognisable one where life is leisurely, and controlled by the rhythms of farming, marketing, and the odd jobs of people like Dede Ikenga. Communal living makes for easy interaction among members of the community as obtains in Laye's *The African Child* and Achebe's *Things Fall Apart*. This is a far cry from the town of Ota with the noise and bustle of its motor park, "Large number of vehicles that went by and the tall buildings which seemed to kiss the horizon . . . long row of shops, kiosks and market stalls" (p. 14). Ota is a typical Nigerian town with running tap water, electricity, imposing public buildings, and a generally enhanced physical development. The human level, apart from the interest of teachers and headmasters in the welfare of their pupils, is relatively undeveloped. Although the Ikengas live in a block of flats among many others, there is no indication that they are acquainted with any other family within the building. Even Nedu's mother refrains from interfering in the goings-on in the Ikenga family; she reprimands Nedu for involving himself in Chisa's problems with his uncle's family.

The major characters in the story are well developed. Chisa is a very well-brought up young boy. Although his mother is illiterate, she instils the principles of morality and discipline in him, trains him to be honest, to work hard, and be efficient. This early training is responsible for his survival through all the vissicitudes during his stay in his uncle's house. It is clearly stated that:

> Chisa did his work well, especially the cleaning and washing up. He had been very well brought up by his mother. His uncle's wife was pleased to have help from him in spite of his tender age (p.26).

Chisa is a model for the younger generation who would do well to emulate his qualities. He is contrasted with his cousin, Dozie Ikenga, who is spoilt and lazy, full of negative tricks, unkindness, like his mother, and cannot pass his examinations. Dozie becomes a liability for his parents who do not know what to do with him. It can be seen that his future is very bleak. Nedu, Chisa's friend is very much like him and this is partly why they become friends. They are both only sons too. Nedu's kindness and friendship sustain Chisa during his travails. They both seem to have the same strict upbringing as revealed in this conversation between them:

> ". . . I am glad I did not do anything wrong or she would have seen me and that would shame me."
> "It is good to do behind others what you would do in front of

them. My mother always said so and she said I should behave as if I am
being watched all the time.

'But it is true. We are being watched by a Supreme Being, whom
we cannot see.'

'Yes, I know that but it is not the same as seeing somebody watching you, is it?'

'Ah, but if I do anything I shouldn't do, she gets very annoyed and
she scolds me and sometimes she beats me.'

'My mother did that too. She did not like me being dirty or lazy. If
I told a lie, even to excuse myself, she would be very angry. I don't like
her being angry so I avoid things she wouldn't want me to do.'

'Did she ever beat you?' asked Nedu.

'Yes, sometimes. . . .' (p. 39).

Kulu's wife is recognizable as a typical narrow-minded, self-
centred woman from whom the modern materialistic life has expung-
ed all humanity, commonsense, and feelings of charitableness. Not
only is she derelict in the upbringing of her children, but she also has
a finely developed criminal propensity which she displays in the
attempt to substitute her lazy son, Dozie, for Chisa in the secondary
schools. Her hold over her husband emanates from the fact that she
has control over the house as it relates to Chisa:

> Chisa dared not complain for fear of bringing his uncle's anger on his
> wife. Somehow, Chisa knew that he would have the sympathy of his
> uncle but he was not in a position to change the situation at home
> because he was not always there. (p. 35).

The relationship between Chisa and his young cousins is plausible, given the stupidity of Dozie and the implacable resentment of
their mother for his presence in their home. Nwakoby uses contrasts
to develop her theme — village contrasted with town, Chisa with
Dozie, Mrs Kulu Ikenga with Nedu's mother, and Mami Ikenga.

On the whole, the village characters emerge with great integrity
and goodness in spite of their lack of material well-being. Town life
tends to corrupt people's feelings as it certainly does to Mrs Kulu
Ikenga, although some people, like young Nedu and his mother survive with their moral feelings intact. *A Lucky Chance* is very well
suited for young readers in the primary and early secondary schools.

With *A House Divided* (Fourth Dimension Publishers, 1985),
Martina Nwakoby makes her debut into the world of adults. Her
story of love, conflict, and prejudice strikes at the heart of a dilemma
with which some of the country's young men and women are faced.
It is the story of Chuma Ochei, a 26 year old Igbo graduate engineer
and Tola Ajayi, a Yoruba pharmacy graduate who, in defiance of old
prejudices and customs which confine marriages within ethnic
boundaries, stake their future on each other, to the consternation

and utter chagrin of their parents and relations. To compound the conflict generated by the situation, the families on both sides have each an alternative, to them more acceptable, marriage candidate for their offspring, from within their own ethnic group. The novel deals with the efforts of each family to bring pressure to bear on their child so as to return them to the accustomed fold, and the young people's steadily growing involvement and understanding of each other and determination to have their way. So adamant are they in their commitment to each other and their vision of their life together that both families eventually surrender to their more persuasive, optimistic pressure. However, just as the issues are being finally resolved in a wedding ritual, tragedy strikes in the murder of the prospective bridegroom.

This story provides the writer with an opportunity to illuminate the various traditions of the two ethnic groups involved in the action — the Igbo and the Yoruba. Common to both is the communal base of society in which an individual is considered only as a miniscule part of a larger organism whose needs take precedence over those of the individual. Tola is very much aware of this and responds to Chuma's proposal with the words:

> "You do not realize the difference in our cultures, Chima. Your people may not accept me as readily as you do and neither would mine."
> "Who cares what they accept as long as we have each other?"
> "It matters, Chima. In this country we still marry families of our spouses whether we like the idea or not . . . (p.40).

Just as Chuma's mother and father attempt to make him fit into the set-up at Odekpe and build on its welfare through the extension of contacts with families and personages within its confines, so Tola's parents, aunts, uncles, cousins and friends try to impress on her obligation to maintain the tradition and well-being of her extended family. Thus, the struggle is one between the desire of the young people to establish their own individual identity, and the insistence of the older generation that the individual identity should be submerged under the claims of society. It is the same struggle depicted in Ogali Ogali's Onitsha market piece, *Veronica my Daughter*. Obi Okonkwo of Achebe's *No Longer At Ease*, faced with the same challenge, succumbed to the claims of parents and society. However, the struggle in *A House Divided* is fiercer on account of the ethnic dimensions. This receives emphasis in the exchange between Chuma and his Yoruba friend, Tunde, in whose flat he had first met Tola:

"Forget her", he said, "You are Igbo and she is Yoruba",

"What do you mean?" retorted Chuma.
"Exactly what I said. You may never see her again.
Tomorrow, you are going back to Ibadan and she remains here."

Tunde was gentle by nature but he understood Chuma's feelings. He was being euphemistic when he added, "As the East is far from the West, Chuma, so are you far from Tola. Differences in culture and background abound." (p.2).

The prejudices which the different tribes hold against each other are highlighted in the drama, very much in the vein of Sidney Poitier's *Guess Who's Coming to Dinner.* Strong elements in each of the cultures, beliefs and traditions also come to light.

Chuma and Tola are separated not only by tribe, but also by their class differences and their societal backgrounds. Tola is introduced as

the youngest of a family of three children, her two elder brothers studying abroad and she the only female. She was very much loved by all who met her for she had a smile for everyone. Pa Ajayi, her father, was an astute businessman who owned a chain of companies engaged in building contracts and supplies and her mother was a wholesale dealer in a locally brewed beer (p.1).

Chuma's middle class upbringing contrasts severely with this, although his good education has opened up bright prospects for him. The rural setting of Chuma's parents' abode also contrasts seriously with the urban environment of Tola's world. Tola's affluent family setting makes her relations feel that she is undertaking senseless degrading step in her bid to marry Chuma. In their estimation, that act would bring disgrace to her family. Generally, the pattern is that a girl improves her financial and social status by marrying into a higher class than hers, and thus enhance her position and that of her relations. The opposite seems to be the case in the relationship between Chuma and Tola, as one of her aunts stresses in desperation to Tola's mother:

How can you be gentle with someone who prefers poverty to riches; a hard narrow bed for a soft one, a cemented floor to a carpeted one? She must be getting out of her mind and it is not being gentle with her that will cure her (p. 96).

The conception of African marriage which centres on the procreation and rearing of children receives attention here. Since in traditional marriage, companionship between the couple is hardly considered, compatibility between husband and wife is of little consequence. Sometimes, the two people concerned, on behalf of whom a marriage is arranged, are ignorant of each other as persons. What matters are the relationships between families and the social position held by the contracting parties. Dele Adeniran, if one is to believe him, has succumbed to such a marriage, claiming that " . . . it was my mother's. She had arranged with this girl's parents to make her my wife. I could not refuse especially after the dowry had been paid and the marriage custom fulfilled. You see, she did everything and I could not back out" (pp. 43–44). A more extreme case is narrated by Chief Kulu:

> "In our days, it was our parents who chose husbands for their daughters and wives for their sons. Times have changed. My own younger sister, was carried to her husband's house by six strong men despite her protests. She scratched them, kicked them, but they overpowered her and took her to the man's house. They stayed around and made sure she remained in his home. My father had arranged the marriage and so it had to take place."
> "And was she happy?"
> "Well, do not ask me such details. But they are still married and have six children," he said triumphantly (pp. 74–75).

Chief Ajose, seeking Tola's hand in marriage on behalf of his medical doctor son, re-enacts the same belief. He expects that his well-established wealth and the friendship which had existed between him and Tola's father should be enough to convince Tola about the advantages of such a union. Chuma's mother, similarly makes several efforts on behalf of her son. One of these involved the young school teacher Njideka who has enough sense to give up when she realizes that Chuma has another girl in his heart. In rejecting Chief Ajose's most attractive offer, Tola insists on the fact: "I have not met your son and he has not seen me. Do not rule out the possibility that he might not like me when he sees me and vice-versa". So the emphasis is on the establishment of mutual understanding, love, and compatibility *before* any serious commitment. The old traditional conception of marriage is one in which a woman is considered as a piece of property that can be of use to whoever acquires her. She is offered as a sacrifice for the promotion of goodwill, contact, or financial advancement of male members of her family. All this is expatiated in Nuruddin Farah's *From a Crooked Rib* and in the novels of Buchi Emecheta.

The new generation, however, is setting up new standards and principles. They insist on appreciation of an individual's character and personality, not necessarily on the size of his purse, extent of property, or the state of the bank account. They think in terms of compatibility, the responses that individuals kindle in each other.

Since people are varied and their tastes differ, the emphasis is on setting up with a person with whom one's characteristics blend; in short, people should come together in marriage if their personalities blend to create harmony. For this, knowledge of the suitors before any talk of marriage is a prerequisite. When Chuma and Tola discuss the subject, their conversation goes like this:

> "Tell me, Tola, if you were to marry, what qualities would you look for in your partner?"
> "Loyalty and kindness," she said without hesitation.
> "Well, good looks and good manners come top of my list," he replied (p. 39).

Tola's conviction that a marriage between her and Chuma would be viable is based on her assessment of him thus:

> He was good looking, and very polite. He was humane. He loved life, loved good music and above all he loved her. He had an independent spirit, was always his own man and did things at his own good pace (p.41).

Thus she bases her choice on matters extraneous to tribe, custom, property, or social status; although, of course, the writer has illuminated very many promising things about him, like

> . . . he had remarkable qualities. As a boy he was the leader of his gang whose members obeyed him because of his charismatic nature. They all seemed to love being bossed by him. At school sports and class work he won awards like the Victor Ludorum Cup and the best Student's Cup. He was strong willed too and nearly took the right decision. (p.3).

Chuma's own appreciation of Tola is based entirely on her person and character. Their fight for the right to marry each other becomes to them one of life and death. It is to the credit of the two families that they are able to realise that human happiness should triumph over material considerations, if it is necessary to pitch the two against each other.

All the characters in this novel come to life, except Dele Adeniran who is used as a foil for the major protagonists. The women are more extremist in their view, illustrating the often perceived fact that women are more conservative than men. Chuma's mother's tenacity and manoeuvres to make him change his mind are based on well-observed details about women of her kind. In each case, the men, perhaps because of their better education and greater exposure to life, are the first to reconcile themselves to new, if challenging, ideas. The geniality of Pa Ajayi and his wife arise from an urbane sophistication that is peculiar to their class.

The two young people, Chuma and Tola, emerge as exceptionally well bred. Their good behaviour, politeness, restraint, avoidance of excesses, their simple desire to give and receive pleasure, make them ideal for emulation by the younger generation. There is none of the coarseness, vulgarity, immorality or amorality with which the younger generation is often identified. To all these are added their strength of character, ability to identify their objectives in life, and to pursue these with single-mindedness, suffering inconvenience (as Tola does when she packs out of her family home in order to assert her right to her own decisions; or Chuma's temporary estrangement from his mother), when necessary. Principled and firm, it is no wonder that they are able to ride successfully the storms of societal opposition, and convert, rather than be converted to succumb to old prejudices.

Martina Nwakoby is very good at descriptions, and she makes her scenes glow with the appropriate choice of words. Her descriptions of furnishings, the placement of decorative items in rooms show a market delicacy, as in her description of the Ajayis' sitting room in Buja:

> The chairs were made of combination of brown upholstery and cloth which complemented the thick lemon carpet that covered the sitting room from wall to wall. The plain white lace curtains that draped the windows rested simply behind the heavy curtains of lemon, mauve and green design. The drinking stools with formica tops had rafia mats on them. There were black and white leather puffs well stuffed with cotton. On the walls hung photographs of members of the family"
> (p.10).

Enugu, the main location of the action in the novel is lovingly presented with its beauties, sites and infirmities. As Chuma and Tola visit the many spots of Enugu — the Zoo, the Hotel Presidential, the Supermarkets, Abakpa Nike, Housing Estate, Achara Layout, the Coal Mines — all these places are brought to life.

The one discordant note in this novel, and one which does violence to its inner dynamics, comes at the end with the murder of Chuma on the day he should have wedded. This pessimistic ending outdoes even Thomas Hardy's well-known propensity. Nothing in the enacted dramatic unfolding of events justifies such an ending. Since the novel has very realistically traced the travails of the young people in overcoming the obstacles to their union (and these are painstakingly delineated, stage by stage), the conclusion, artistically, would have been a resolution by a happy ending. This would have been more in consonance with all the arguments within the novel — an appreciation of the individuals' claim to personal happiness, and the opening up of new vistas to better understanding and relationship between the various ethnic groups in Nigeria (whose cultures, when seen at close quarters have more similarities than differences). The dashing of these'hopes through the murder of Chuma has two artistic implications. Either the writer is repudiating the seemingly progressive arguments she has proffered in the body of the novel by suggesting that a union between Chuma and Tola is ill-advised and that the ethnic misunderstandings and prejudices should continue, or she is implying that all which has transpired in the novel so far has been an illusion, a fairy-tale, and that the murder brings the reader back to reality. That might in fact be the objective which harmonizes with the title of the novel *A House Divided*. However, neither of these can be sustained when the totality of the novel — plot, emerging theme, setting, characterisation — is taken into account.

Although the prime suspect of the murder, Dele Adeniran, is a jealous, frustrated man, his overall character, the fact that he is already married and thus renounced legitimate claims to Tola's affection, especially when he had initially an opportunity to marry her but failed to take advantage of it, makes it difficult, within the novel's framework, to accept Chuma's murder as an artistic resolution of his bitterness. Dele Adeniran has been presented as a self-loving, easygoing man of the world who is quite popular with the ladies. If the writer is to make him true of himself, he should have quite easily consoled himself with another girl. The question is not whether such a thing cannot happen. Of course, it can happen. But we are here dealing with art, not raw life. Certain things have to cohere to achieve the internal dynamics of a work of art.

On the whole, then, *A House Divided* is a delightful, highly entertaining novel which highlights efforts by the younger generation to forget the prejudices of their elders, and to weld a more unified country through appreciation of each other on the basis of individual merit. It projects good ideals and principles for the young and the old. It is, however, marred by the imposition of an artistically faulty unhappy ending.

MARTINA AWELE NWAKOBY

Born 12 March 1937 in Ogwashi-Uku, Bendel State. Educated at Holy Child Convent School, Anua, Uyo, Akwa Ibom State, 1947–51; Cornelia Connelly College, Uyo, 1952–1958; Holy Rosary Training College, Enugu, 1958–1959; The Library School, College of Commerce Gosta Green, Birmingham England, 1964–1966, obtaining Associate of Library Association (ALA) London Certificate; Has a Master of Library Science (MLS) degree from the University of Pittsburgh 1974 and Ph.D in Library Studies from the University of Ibadan, 1984. Has held numerous positions in the Library profession both at home and abroad, including Librarian, former College of Technology, Enugu, 1973. President, Nigerian Library Association, Anambra State Division, 1977–1979; Vice-President, Business and Professional Women's Club, Enugu Branch, 1979 to date. Honoured with the membership of Beta Phi Mu (an International Library honour society) in 1975. Listed in "World Who's Who of Women", 1977 edition. First prize winner of the 1978 Macmillan Children's book competition, 1979. Has held non-executive directorship of many companies including being a Director, First City Merchant Bank, Lagos, from 1984 to date. She is married, with four children, to Patrick Oguejiofor Nwakoby and currently lecturing at the Imo State University, Etiti Campus, Imo State, Nigeria.

Publications

Ten in the Family, London: Evans, 1977
A Lucky Chance. Ibadan: Macmillan, 1980
Quiz Time, Enugu: Nwamife Press, 1980
A House Divided. Enugu: Fourth Dimension, 1985

Others

Library Education In West Africa

Articles

"Promoting Reading Habits in Children." *Bulletin of Information* (2 & 3), April/December 1978

Unpublished Articles

"Books for All" (Paper presented at the Annual Conference of the Nigerian Library Association, 1975)
"Children's Reading Habits' (Paper presented at the Ife Book Fair 1978)
The Role of Libraries in Research and Development" (Paper presented at the Nigerian Library Association Conference in 1985).

Chapter 14

Helen Ofurum's
A Welcome for Chijioke
Henrietta C. Otokunefor

A Welcome for Chijioke, which is Ofurum's second book in the Macmillan Winners' Series for boys and girls, is a 92-page tragi-comedy. It is the story of Chijioke Igwe, an eleven year old boy who, after the tragedy of his mother's death, went in search of his father whom he has never seen and knew little about. The setting was in the village of Adamoka where he lived a happy and intimate life with his mother:

> Chijioke and his mother were very close. He was her only child and he loves her dearly. Chijioke was eleven years old and had spent all of his eleven years living with his mother in the village of Adamoka. (p.2).

His mother, known by the villagers as Mama Chijioke, was an industrious, sympathetic, and a likeable woman, who passed on to her only son and child the good qualities of hardwork, respect for elders and a good sense of responsibility. She ran a small eating house. This life of love and intimacy was soon severed by the death of Chijioke's mother.

There is a great similarity here between Martina Nwakoby's Chisa in her *A Lucky Chance* and Chijioke. Chisa was taken away from his village, Omonda, and his parents where he had a secure, happy life of love and intimacy by his uncle, Kulu.

Before her death, Chijioke's mother gave him two photographs of herself and his father respectively; a letter and some money. She also told him that his father, whose name is Gabriel Okezie, an engineer with a big company, lives in Lagos and that he should find him.

Chijioke was taken to Onitsha by his mother's sister, Mrs Anya, after his mother's death. He was not happy in the Aunt's house. Mr Anya (the Aunt's husband) and the children did not want him and treated him like a servant.

> Mr Anya continued to treat Chijioke like a servant, much to his wife's annoyance. However, she was not able to do anything about it. The children noticed their father's treatment of Chijioke and this encouraged them to treat him likewise when their mother was not around.

(p. 15).

Chisa in Nwakoby's *A Lucky Chance* received the same type of treatment from his uncle's wife and from Dozie his cousin. Chijioke had to run away to Lagos aided by Sylvester (Mrs Anya's houseboy) when he could no longer stay in his Aunt's house. Before he left Onitsha for Lagos, Sylvester had earlier written to his brother, Matthew Eze, who agreed to board Chijioke while in Lagos. Two days after his arrival in Lagos, Sylvester joined him having lost his job as a result of Chijioke's flight. Chijioke set out to accomplish his one mission of finding his father in Lagos. The search was a very tedious one. Many times, he almost gave up having suffered a lot of setback:

> Chijioke stopped searching as he realised that it was like looking for a needle in a haystack. He wondered, as on so many other occasions, whether he would ever find his father. Perhaps the best thing for him to do would be to go back to his aunt's house and apologise for causing her so much trouble. But when he thought of how unhappy he was when he stayed there, he felt that anything was better than to return (p.70).
>
> After some time, Chijioke felt as if the walls of the building were closing in on him, so he decided to go out for some fresh air. He had been walking along the road for a while, thinking about his problems, when there was a shout from behind him. 'Get out of the way!' And before Chijioke could move, he was hit with force by a bicycle on the back of the legs and thrown to the ground. For a moment, he lay stunned, not knowing what had happened. (p.70).

He finally met his father in a most unusual circumstance. "Nda" Sylvester and Matthew had taken Chijioke to the Bar Beach on Sunday to cheer him up. Mr Okezie had taken his family to the Bar Beach instead of Tarkwa Bay to accommodate some emergency business meeting. A near tragedy loomed as Nkechi was swept away by a huge wave. Chijioke, without consideration for personal safety, jumped in to rescue Nkechi from the angry waves and presented her to the father. But as he took Nkechi from this heroic stranger with many thanks,

> . . . Their eyes met and for a moment the world seemed to stand still for both of them. Mr Okezie saw himself as he was when he was young. Chijioke saw the man whose photograph he had carried around with him for so many months. (p.82).

Chijioke was given a hero's welcome into the Okezie family following the circumstances of their meeting. The family, comprising father, mother, and three daughters made his absorption so natural and easy.

> Good morning. My name is Nkechi. I am your little sister. I want to
> thank you for saving my life. It is so nice to have a big brother. Perhaps,
> now that you are around, Chioma and Nneka won't bully me so much.
> (p.90).
> Good morning, Chijioke. We have just come to say welcome to you.
> You were very brave to jump into the sea like that and save Nkechi.
> (p.90).
> I am so lucky to have found my father and to have such a good
> stepmother, he thought to himself. They and my sisters have welcomed
> me from the bottom of their hearts. If only my mother could see me
> now, she would be so happy for me. (p.92).

What a contrast to the cold welcome he got from the Anya family at
Onitsha.

A Welcome For Chijioke is deeply rooted in the physical and
cultural Nigerian society that the average Nigerian boy or girl will be
able to identify with. Helen Ofurum uses her characters as the vehicles for her message by contrasting them.

Chijioke's mother, a rural-dweller is contrasted with her sister,
Mrs Anya, an urban-dweller. While the former takes time to train her
only child and son, the latter fails to do the same for her children:

> His mother had always said to him, 'Chijioke, never be unkind. Always
> give to those less fortunate than yourself.' Chijioke always remembered
> his mother's advice and it was now always in his nature to be kind and
> thoughtful. (p.7).

The result of this difference is further contrasted in the behaviour of their children. Chijioke, the hero of the story is contrasted
with his cousin Uzoma. Both boys are of the same age but are
remarkably different in behaviour. Mr Anya, a busy Onitsha businessman thinks it is just enough to have children well fed and clothed:

> Mr Anya was a fat, bad-tempered businessman who travelled quite a lot.
> He was always busy and did not have time to sit down and talk with his
> children. However, he always makes sure that they were fed and
> clothed and he felt this was enough. (p.11).

What a contrast to Mr Gabriel Okezie, an engineer in a large company
in Lagos who is never too busy to spend some time with his children
in addition to providing for them.

> Mr Gabriel Okezie (who was also Chijioke's father) loved his children
> dearly. Although he was an engineer in a large company in Lagos, he
> was never too busy for his children. When he returned from work, he

would call the children and ask how they had spent their day. If the children had any problems, he would try to help to solve them. (p.27).

In contemporary Nigeria, the youths are castigated for throwing overboard the Nigerian or African tradition of respect for elders and the institution of African extended family culture. Chijioke's thoughtfulness, kindness, perseverance, obedience and show of respect for elders clearly reflect the upbringing by a gentle, industrious, sympathetic and loving mother. The author appears to be saying that the child more or less reflects the home. Chijioke has respect for his elders because of the training he got from his mother who, for the short time they spent together, took time to instruct him accordingly.

A Welcome For Chijioke is presented in a clear simple lucid English using short chapters and in a narrative form. Although on three occasions, the author starts a sentence and even a paragraph with the word *'because'*, the work is a valuable reading material for boys and girls of late primary and early secondary schools, respectively. It makes for light reading.

HELEN O. OFURUM

Born 12 November 1941, in Scotland, by a British mother and a Nigerian father. Had her primary education in Nigeria and secondary education in Scotland. Attended the Scottish College of Commerce (now University of Strathclyde) in Glasgow. Married with four children. Currently working as an accountant for the Hardel and Enic Group of Companies in Owerri, Imo State, Nigeria.

Publications

"Theoma Comes to Stay (Winners Series-Macmillan).
A Welcome for Chijioke" 1983 (Winners Series-Macmillan).

Chapter 15

Mary Okoye on Juvenile Detective Story
Obiageli C. Nwodo

There is a general dearth of local reading materials for children and young adults in the Nigerian literary market. However, some local publishers are trying to reverse the situation. One of such is the Macmillan Nigeria Limited. Under its "Winners Series", interesting as well as captivating fiction stories have been released.

Kukoro-koo[1] by Mary Okoye is one of such titles in the series. It is an exciting detective story about a group of children from a village called Ogoeke. They call themselves the Secret Council and Kukoro-koo is their secret signal for beckoning each other for some urgent discussion. As the need for a girls' secondary school became increasingly evident in Ogoeke, the community leaders decided to build one but not without some hitches. These brilliant kid characters realizing early enough that someone somewhere was determined to sabotage the community's efforts, quickly went to work with great detective zeal, dealing with the problems with skilful manoeuvres and finally unearthing the secret that lay inside the locked gate of the mystery compound.

This exciting eighty-two page story has an engaging theme of crime and detection. It is compact, fast-moving and a real moral for both the young and the old.

The story unfolds within a community in a typical Eastern Nigerian local government area. There is a bit of indecision here for the author could not make up her mind as to the temporary setting of the story. At times, one feels that the events or actions must have taken place in the pre-civil war era — 'Mango' having passed the night in "PWD yard" instead of the current Ministry of Works. At other times the plot begins to take on some contemporary outlook; for instance, Chief Uzodinma's house is said to have been built long before the civil war, implying that the story was told after the civil war. The same Chief complains about not having many girls' schools in the local government area. The author talks about 'Kombi bus', '504 station wagon' and officials from the local government headquarters at Aduru coming for the launching ceremony, all these wearing contemporary flavour of the post-civil war era.

The above notwithstanding, what we have is a detective story with a difference. We are not unsure as to 'who's done it' but only anxious as to how soon the secret council will uncover the culprit. Right from the start, an accusing finger is pointed: "But you know, that Okafor man is wicked" says Joe. (p.5).

The community discussed is not a community without some problems. There are as divergent views as there are opinions. When the idea of a Girls' Secondary School was muted, not only was choosing a site a problem but some felt that a 'Social Club', a 'town hall' and even a 'hotel' should have been built first. This again points to an Igbo social climate in which each individual thinks that his or her opinion is as good if not better than the other's opinion. Chief Uzodinma whose interest was the development of his community was on hand to give his reasons why Ogoeke should have a girls' school:

> "There are no other girls' schools nearby and the one in Aduru is not even big enough for Aduru alone. The Government wants more girls' schools. In this area many boys go on to secondary school, but most girls stop at primary six". (p.11).

The chief appreciates the value of girls' education; two of his daughters having benefited from it, and are now a teacher and a nurse respectively. Ogoeke needed more of these educated girls in the community. A situation where most girls ended in primary six will not yield this needed result.

In actual fact then, Ogoeke was a community in transition. Transition from the age-old tradition of unequal opportunity among boys and girls. Education for the boys was considered a dire necessity whereas that for the girls was considered unnecessary or a luxury. Those were the days. It is interesting to note however, that while this was the situation some years back, the pendulum has now swung in favour of girls, not only in secondary but also in university education. Hence, the Anambra State Secondary School enrolment statistics for 1985/86 academic year indicated 61% to 30% in favour of girls. What a whopping difference! Times have indeed changed.

One other aspect of Igbo tradition that was dealt with is the spirit of communal self-help. It is a deeply rooted tradition practised in Igbo-land from time immemorial. While it is employed at various levels among different communities, Abriba people were known to have used it for "collection of crops, harvesting of communal palm-fruits, building of log-bridges and houses as well as construction and maintenance of footpaths, markets and village squares"[2]. When one of the conditions to be fulfilled before the school site could be approved, required clearing of land and putting up some of the buildings, the people naturally turned to this time-tested tradition, not only for clearing the land but also for generating funds for the building. Ogoeke women were not left out. They "promised to fetch all the water that would be needed for the building of the school". (p.51).

While others were performing their civic responsibility, Okafor decided to double-cross his people. He represents a typical corrupt Nigerian, selfish, unreliable, boastful and highly unpredictable. He withholds information about the conditions for the approval of the school site; he diverted the officials to the wrong site and to make matters worse, demanded and got ₦500 (five hundred naira) as a "gift" to the ministry officials. This we later learnt he used for bribing the officials to divert the materials to his private property.

In Nigerian society today, there are so many faces of Mr Okafor. Their stocks-in-trade are, reaping where they did not sow, making millions without the corresponding effort, building hotels, estates, dream houses with money stolen from the common coffers, mounting the rostrum at launching ceremonies to declare their ill-gotten wealth. Okafor was a real tribalist and a crook, an opportunist who abused his position as the secretary of the building committee. The author in developing his character was actually portraying for us not a particular person but a person belonging to a particular class of social plague.

While the author captures in the character of Mr Okafor the real corrupt Nigerian, she makes an idol out of Mr Amadi, the headmaster. He represents everything that Okafor is not. He is interested in the welfare of the community despite his not being "son of the soil". He proved supportive and understanding to the problems presented to him by the detective bunch. He was straightforward and meticulous, this he later demonstrated when he compelled the children to clean-up the launching ground after the exercise. He was a trustworthy friend whose judicious handling of Mango's revelation brought about tracking down the culprit, Mr Okafor.

What really makes the story fascinating is the role played by the young detective bunch. These characters are very well developed. Peter, the Chairman of the 'Secret Council' is a "Snow Ball' *(Animal Farm)* type of character. He is clever, tactful, resourceful and has an answer to almost all their problems. To get at vital information, he suggests to Joe to fake stomach ache; to get Mr Amadi, the headmaster to help them with their problems, he tells him just "enough to explain why they are "worried and need his help" (p.31) but nothing more.

Joy, the sister, on the other hand, is portrayed as a hardworking girl, dedicated to duty and academically sound. She is very obedient to her parents (p.26) and unlike the brother, Peter, does all the household chores.

Joe, the information officer, is an orator, very inquisitive, highly vigilant and with a keen sense of perception. He goes at all length to get information even when his own life is at stake. He hates Mr Okafor with passion and it is through him actually that the story is told.

Mango, the caretaker of the 'Council den', is a real snooper and a truant. He is as contemplative as he is curious, and very determined to get at the secret of the mystery compound even at the risk of his own life. He proved courageous, tactful and without him the mystery might not have been uncovered. One might object that the story is not true to life since these children are made to think and act at a level higher than their normal age. However, it is not unusual to see this precocity, as anybody who has read Anne Blyden's series would testify to such.

In general, the pictures and instincts depicted are real and true of African village setting — Mango cupping his hands under his plate to warm-up himself (p.71). The description of Chief Uzodinma's house; the "soft grass slope" near the Nzu stream where the school is to be built; the scene describing the burning of the site with "the red tongues of flame leaping upwards towards the sky" (p.37). The "pieces of charred black glass caught by the wind; the small animals driven out from the shelter of the grass by the heat; the birds of prey, vultures, black kite, circling in the air, hovering and watching for a chance to pounce on an unlucky victim" (p.37–38) — all reminiscent of scenes from Cyprian Ekwensi's *Burning Grass*.

But one cannot help noticing the cultural misrepresentation in the passage where the author insists that the night-watchman be called by his first name, Mango. This is considered a mark of disrespect for elders and unguarded upbringing in Igbo traditional culture.

In all, the story is true to life. The words are simple and arranged in pleasant patterns. The illustrations are clear and precise. The theme depicts some special aspect of human experience and the greatest pleasure and satisfaction derived in the work lie in the fact that it brings one back to the realities of human situations, problems, feelings and relationships. Children between the ages of 9–13 will find this an enjoyable leisure reading.

References

1. Okoye, Mary; *Kukoro-koo!* Ibadan: Macmillan, 1982. Further references to this text will be to this edition and will be incorporated in the body of the article and placed in brackets.
2. Osuji, Emman E., "Rural Development by Self-Help Effort in Abriba, Imo State Nigeria". *Nigeria Magazine* No. 147, p.57.

MARY OKOYE

Is of British parentage and a Nigerian citizen by marriage. A science graduate who taught at Queen's School Enugu, 1961–1973. Transferred to the Ministry of Education, Enugu, where she worked and rose to the rank of Chief Inspector of Education. Obtained a doctorate degree in Education, 1985. Married to a lawyer, with four (4) children. She enjoys reading, puzzles of all kinds and sewing. Presently seeking new employment as lecturer in education.

Publications

Kukoro-koo! Ibadan: Macmillan, 1980:
Co-author of *Science: Step by Step,* (a primary science text book series of 3 books and 3 teachers guides, Ibadan. Macmillan, 1976–78.
Nwankwo and the Secret Council. Ibadan: University Press(Forthcoming).
Mr. Ude's New Bus. Ibadan: University Press (Forthcoming).

Unpublished work

Papa Joseph's New Bed. (A short story read by B.B.C. World Service November, 1979).

CHARRY ADA ONWU

Publications

Catastrophe. Akure: Fagbamigbe Publishers,
Ifeanyi and Obi (Children's Literature)
One Bad Turn. Akure: Fagbamigbe

Works in Press with Longman Publishers

Mama's Love
Our Grannies Tales
Tales of Tragedies
Tit more Tat

Review

One Bad Turn Deserves . . . . . . Reviewed in *The Guardian* (Lagos) 25 November 1986, p.13. *Reviewer* Ezeani, Andy.

ANJI OSSAI

Publication

Tolulope. Walton-On-Thames: Nelson, 1979.

HELEN AIYEOHUSA OVBIAGELE

Born in Benin City in the forties. Educated at C.M.S. Girls School, Benin City, St. Peter's College, Kaduna, College of Education, Lagos Universities of Lagos and South Kensington, London. Taught at the Lagos City College Yaba, Lagos and Corona School, Ikoyi, Lagos. Worked with Peugeot Automobile Nigeria Ltd. Currently working with Vanguard Media Ltd.

Publications

Evbu my love 1980
A fresh Start, 1982
You Never Know, 1982
Forever Yours, 1985.

Chapter 16

Mabel Segun: A Critical Review*

Funso Aiyejina

Mabel Segun, *nee* Aig-Imoukuede, who has also written and published as Mabel Jolaoso, is a multi-talented individual who has made
her mark as a pioneer in several fields including sports, general and
educational broadcasting, editing, information, teaching and creative
writing. Her pioneering spirit which led her, as the first female table
tennis player in Nigeria, to enter for Men's Singles, is evident in
several facets of her life such as the tenacious production and promotion of children's literature for which she has become widely known
and respected.

She graduated from the University College, Ibadan in 1953 as a
member of the first generation of indigenously educated Nigerian
graduates from among whom most of Nigeria's celebrated creative
writers emerged. She is at present a Senior Research Fellow in the
University of Ibadan's Institute of African Studies.

The critical attention given to Mabel Segun to date has been
grossly disproportionate to her creative output. This critical neglect is consequent on a number of reasons, one being the fact that literary criticism in Nigeria is still substantially a male affair and more
often than not, only a nodding acknowledgement is granted the female writer. More specifically, however, is the fact that, although she
has been represented in several local and international journals, magazines and anthologies and translated into several international languages, a lot of her works have not been collected. Her substantial output
in the area of children's literature also remains unacknowledged by
critics who are generally, and unfortunately, apathetic about children's literature. In addition, while most Nigerian writers, except the
outstandingly versatile few, concentrate on specific genres or sub-
genres, Mabel Segun has spread herself too thinly over several areas.

In *Sorry, No Vacancy* (1985), a collection of some of her satirical

*A slightly different version of this essay was published in the "Guardian Literary Series",
The Guardian (Lagos), Saturday, August 2, 1986, p. 13.

radio broadcasts made between 1961 and 1974, originally published as *Friends, Nigerians, Countrymen* (1977), she paints a rib-tickling picture of several aspects of Nigerian life, based principally on her own experiences and (mis) adventures at home and abroad. Her lively and conversational style, her ability to surprise with her deductions and the ease with which she fuses disparate aspects of life combine to give this collection its distinctive character. Her stance in these sketches is as self-critical and self-mocking as it is critical of societal foibles and ethos. She lambasts both ceremonial fops and self-deluding members of the society as well as institutionalized habits while also chastizing the writer's observing ego.

The sense of adventure, the didactic overlay in *Sorry, No Vacancy* and the humorous tone with which she portrays otherwise grim topics and events are positively utilized in her books for children where their combination is employed to retain the attention of the target audience. As a writer of books for children and as a promoter of children's literature, she has demonstrated a concern for the recreational and educational value of books in the overall development of children as emotionally balanced, intellectually alert and culturally rooted citizens.

In her autobiographical reader for children, *My Father's Daughter* (1965), she captures the essence of life in a small, rural society at the transitional stage between an animist past and a technological future. Unlike most of the works set in transitional African societies, however, the emphasis in *My Father's Daughter* is not the stock-in-trade culture-clash. Even though she presents evidence of the incursion of western religious belief and habits, her main focus is on the balance which the community strives to achieve between man and nature, between man and man, regardless of differences in religious or cultural belief, and between parents and their offspring. In consonance with this approach, the narrator's father who functions as the village pastor, peace-maker, dispenser and disciplinarian dominates the world-view of the child-narrator and emerges as the positive guiding and unifying spirit in her emergent consciousness. Mabel Segun employs a clear, effective and plausible prose style and, while the whole work possesses a narrative unity, each chapter is so self-contained that it is possible for children to assimilate it in manageable proportions. More importantly, while never losing sight of the didactic role of children's books, an endearing sense of humour pervades the entire work. One of the most memorable scenes in this book deals with the thieves who having raided the pastor's house, hide out in the bush to avoid detection. They nearly get away until the alarm clock which they have stolen goes off and reveals their location!

In addition to *My Father's Daughter,* Mabel Segun has published four other books for children: *Under the Mango Tree,* Books 1 and 2, (1980) which she co-edited with Neville Grant, *Youth Day Parade* (1984) and *Olu and the Broken Statue* (1985). The *Under the Mango Tree* set contains traditional songs and poems from all over the world, with emphasis on Africa and the diaspora, which have been selected for both their entertainment value and their didactic nature. *Youth Day Parade* is the story of Tunde who has been appointed by his headmaster to organize his fellow pupils for a Youth Day Parade. Although Tunde is initially daunted by the enormity of the assignment, through consultations with other pupils and as a result of the consequent collective planning, he manages to put together a first-rate performance. In this 22-page story, Mabel Segun manages, without being overbearing, to highlight the need for citizens to be patriotic, self-reliant and nationalistic rather than ethnic in their approach to their civic duties. Her characters, for example are named with a deliberateness which is faithful to the ethnic plurality of the nation.

The fourth book, *Olu and the Broken Statue,* is her most impressive book for children to date. This book tells the story of Olu, Ikem and Aigbe, three members of one of the teams set up by their headmaster for the purpose of doing odd jobs in exchange for donations to be used for purchasing new musical instruments for their School Band. Since a benefactor has promised to match their total collection with an equivalent donation, the headmaster promises a silver cup, as an incentive, to the team which collects the largest amount of money. The story highlights inter-team rivalries as well as intra-team misunderstanding and co-operation. There is the occasional temptation to cheat but the pupils always remember their headmaster's injunction not to do anything against the law. The final test of their sense of responsibility and patriotism as well as their ability to take initiative is provided by their discovery of an ancient bronze statue. They are faced with the option of either selling it for a few hundred *naira* to tourists and winning the silver cup or taking it to the museum in accordance with government's directive thus helping to preserve the ancient heritage of the country. After a debate of their options, they decide to take the statue to the museum in spite of their desire to win the cup. They attend the prize-giving ceremony hoping to place third or second, especially since they have found out that at least one other team has collected more money than their own total. Unknown to them however, in appreciation of their honesty and patriotism, the director of the museum makes a substantial donation in their names thus making theirs the winning team.

The major strength of this book is the unobstrusive manner in which the writer's didacticism is sublimated within the story. This is achieved through a deliberate projection of a variety of adventures which highlight different types of possibilities from which the boys must make a choice. Each adventure provides the boys with new options and new possibilities thus making them cumulatively wiser. In addition, the story is rooted in a physical and cultural terrain with which the average African child will be able to identify.

Since 1953 when Mabel Segun won the first prize in the National Festival of the Arts with a short story — "The Surrender" — about campus life, she has written many more short stories, some of which have appeared in the *Sunday Times, Modern Woman, West African Review, Nigeria Magazine* and in a number of anthologies. In some of these short stories, especially in those that deal with superstition, she acts as a faithful chronicler while in others she displays a critical approach to such belief. "The Legacy" is an example of the first type. A self-confessed witch is dying a tortured death. She asks to see her only daughter and the villagers refuse to grant her request because they are afraid that she would transfer her witchcraft to her daughter. Just as she is about to die, her daughter unsuspectingly walks into the death-chamber and into her mother's embrace. Outside, the crowd waits to see the child-witch emerge. Mabel Segun does not intervene, she merely documents. But in "Terror of the Hoodoo", she resolves the story in such a manner as to cause the reader to question the efficacy of superstition. The story is about a bridegroom who lives in the shadow of the belief that since he had fallen from his mother's back when he was a baby, his bride will die and that he will lose a total of four wives through death before the curse becomes impotent. Ayodele, the brigdegroom, protects his wife from every conceivable harm, not because he loves her, but because he does not want the curse on him confirmed. However, in spite of his care and efforts, he loses her; not to death but to a rich businessman!

Many of Mabel Segun's short stories are set in urban areas and explore urban issues such as rootlessness, materialism and a disdain for rural concepts and habits. Her stories are replete with disillusioned, suicidal and uprooted characters who usually narrowly miss the final leap into oblivion. In "Bola", she demonstrates that the rural character who turns her back on her roots and uncritically embraces the fast life of the city is bound to suffer both physical and psychological distress.

As in the case of her short stories, her poems have also appeared in several journals and anthologies. But while her short stories remain, rather unfortunately, uncollected, her poems have been collected under the title of *Conflict and Other Poems* (1986). Although some of her poems date back to 1952, they speak pointedly to the present and are as socially anchored as most of the best poetry written by contemporary Nigerian poets. Even when her subject matter is dated as in the treatment of the Sharpeville massacre in the poems "A Second Olympus" and "Impotence", her vision is commendable because it is usually perceptive and prophetically appropriate as evidenced in the current turmoil in South Africa where "fermenting hate" has at last pushed out the restraining "cork". Her most celebrated poem, "Conflict", which has been included in about six anthologies, is a prototype of the schizophrenic state of the colonial. The despondent "but where can I go?" of this poem echoes one of the central questions which continue to punctuate our life and literature in the search for personal and group identities since our contact with the outside world. Describing the tragedy and dilemma of the colonial, she affirms:

> Here I stand
> infant overblown
> poised between two civilizations,
> finding the balance irksome,
> itching for something to happen,
> to tip us one way or the other
> groping in the dark for a helping hand
> and finding none.
>
> ("Conflict")

Most of the poems in *Conflict and Other Poems* look at various aspects of our "development" since the contact with the outside world and the efforts, mostly futile, made in order to resolve the conflicts generated by that contact. She wonders "which part of me will be supreme —/ the old and tested one, the present/or the future unknown?" ("The Pigeon-Hole"). Her attempt to answer this question in these poems reveals that the past, while being duly acknowledged, should not be romanticized and the present with its political, social and economic contradictions, and as a catalyst of the future, must remain the central focus of our endeavours. Although her ideological stance may not be as 'revolutionary' as that of the new crop of 'revolutionary' writers, especially the feminists, her reading of the society is incisive, profound and eloquent. She aptly portrays politicians as "the smart ones/ who squeeze blood out of stone/..... who rob the nation's treasury/And get honoured for it". ("The Smart One"). They "curdled the milk and saddened the honey/And turned the land to desolation" ("Corruption") such that today;

The leaves are blowing about the land
And the air is filled with a smell of rot,
And wriggly forms are dancing about
On this dunghill that was our land ....
It is a feast of maggots.

("Corruption")

In the face of such a decadent ethos and in a world from where justice has flown and human rights have become "A mere torrent of words at meetings/And a deluge of paperwork/With resolutions/Signifying nothing", the need to search for an alternative is as self-evident as it is inevitable. As the society is poised for this search, the poet warns against the danger inherent in any attempt to trust our future to self-proclaimed messiahs who are out only to save (for) themselves. ("The Messiahs"). In essence, she advocates the view that a messianic vision is not a viable alternative to our present predicament of false starts and predictable falls which yield nothing but "A horizon receding/Perpetually receding/The more we approached it" ("A Horizon Receding"). She never really proffers an alternative, and this does not detract from the overall impact of her poetry, especially since the precise portrayal of the society in these poems is so compelling that the reader cannot but think of positive alternatives.

Stylistically, Mabel Segun's poetry is accessible and direct without being simplistic and she is an effective user of irony and macabre humour. She also employs narrative techniques in a number of her poems such that they come across as tales told in verse. When she succeeds with these techniques, the outcome is usually compelling and commendable as in "Human Torches" and "Musical Chairs" but when, as in "Rainmaker", she does not, the outcome is anticlimactic.

Taken together, Mabel Segun's subtly hilarious and iconoclastic essays, poetry, short stories (which one hopes will soon be collected) and, especially, books for children have secured her a place in Nigerian literature.

MABEL DOROTHY SEGUN

Nee Aig-Imoukhuede, born February 18, 1930 in Ondo State. Attended C.M.S. Girls' School, Lagos and obtained Cambridge School Certificate in 1947; B.A. (London) in English, Latin and History at the University College, Ibadan in 1953. Short Courses: Publicity and Public Relations (London 1962), Printing, typography, media selection (Lagos 1964) and Book Editing (New York 1965–66). Attachment: Silver Burdett (Morristown, New Jersey 1965), Harper and Row (New York 1966).

As a teacher, she is quite experienced. Between June 1953 and now she taught English, Latin and History in such renowned educational institutions as St. Anne's School, Ibadan; Methodist Girls' High School, Yaba; Government College, Benin City; Government Teacher Training College, Abraka; Ibadan Boys' High School; Corona School, Yaba; National Technical Teachers' College, Yaba. As a broadcaster, between 1967 and 1970, she worked in the Broadcasting Unit, Federal Ministry of Education, Lagos. Hansard Editor for both Houses of the Western Region Legislature, July 1958—March 1961. Copywriter, Links (West Africa) Limited, Lagos. Editor, "Modern Women", Lagos, December 1964—September 1965, August 1966—February 1967. Freelance writing and broadcasting and Freelance editor, March—August 1966. Editor, Franklin Book Programmes, Lagos, February—May 1967. Associate Editor, "BookBird", Vienna, Austria, 1978—79. Editor of ten books produced at the African Children's Writers Workshop, Nairobi, Kenya, 1984. Deputy Permanent Delegate of Nigeria to Unesco, Paris, July 1979—September 1981. Member, National Commission on Right Hand Traffic 1970—72, National Sports Commission 1971—1975. Associate Member, Institute of Public Relations, London, 1965—66; Member, International Board on Books for Young People (IBBY) 1978—79, 1984—86. Founder and President, Children Literature Association of Nigeria (CLAN), 1978—present. Chairman, International Year of the Child (IYC). Member, Association of Nigerian Authors (ANA), 1982 to the present. Celebrated Table Tennis star and very active sportswoman with numerous National and International awards. Member of numerous sports organisations. A mother of three. Currently, Senior Research Fellow (Publications), Institute of African Studies, University of Ibadan, Nigeria.

Publications (Books)

My Father's Daughter. Lagos: African University Press, 1965
Friends, Nigerians, Countrymen. Ibadan: Oxford University Press, 1971.
Co-authored with Neville Grant, *Under the Mango Tree*, Books I and 2(poetry). Longmans, 1980.
Youth Day Parade. Ibadan: DUCA, 1983.
My Mother's Daughter. Ibadan: African University Press, 1985.
Olu and the Broken Statue. Ibadan: New Horn Press, 1985.
Conflict and Other Poems. Ibadan: New Horn Press, 1986.

Others

Poems in *Schwarzer Orpheus* - edited by Janheinz John (in German), Published by Carl Verlag, Munchen, 1954.

Poems and short stories in *Christ Erscheint am Kongo,* edited by Peter Sulzer (in German), published by Eugen Salzer, Verlag Heilbronn, 1958; Poems and essays in *Reflections,* edited by Frances Ademola, Lagos, U.A.P., 1968.

Poems in *Black African Voices,* Illinois, Scott Foresman, Glenview, 1970.

Poems in *Poems from Africa.* Boston: Thomas Y. Cronwell, 1973.

Poems in *African Writing: A Thematic Anthology.* London: William Collins, 1974.

Poem in *Success in Reading Book 7,* Silver Burdett (Now General Learning Corporation), Morristown, N.J., 1973.

Poem in *Worlds of English, Book 2.* Oslo, Norway: Glydendal Norsk Forlag, 1975.

"Book Development in Nigeria since Independence: Problems, Policies, Programmes, and Prospects" in *Independent Nigeria:* The first 25 years (forthcoming).

"One Unesco, Many Voices" - (unpublished).

Published Papers/Articles

"The African Child of Today and the World of Books: the need for cultural Identity". Being Report of the 17th Congress of the International Board on Books for Young People (IBBY), Prague, 1980.

"Book Development Problems in Developing Countries with special reference to Modern Realistic stories for Young People", 16th IBBY Congress, Wurzburg, Arbeitskreis fur Jugen literature e.v. Murrieh, 1978, 198p.

"Book Production and Distribution in Nigeria," 19th IBBY Congress, Nicosia, Cyprus, 1984.

Aig-Imoukhuede, Mabel "On Being a West African Writer", Ibadan, November 12, 1961 p.12.

"Organising Writing Workshops" being report of the Commonwealth African Book Development Seminar, Ibadan, Nigeria, 2—14 February, 1975, 41—46p.

Others

"Character-Building Books for Young People". Being a paper presented at the 6th Annual Curriculum Textbooks Exhibition and Workshop on Writing for Youths: Education Library, University of Lagos, April 15—18, 1985.

"The Image of old age in Nigerian Children's Literature". Paper presented at the Institute of African Studies Seminar, University of Ibadan, Ibadan, on 22 May, 1985.

"The Literary Contribution of Nigerian Women Writers". Paper Presented at the Conference on the "The Contribution of Women to National Development," Nigerian Association of University Women. United States Information Service, Lagos, 3—4 June, 1985.

"A survey of, and comments on, books produced by Nigerian authors". Being a paper presented at the Lagos State Library Service Workshop on the Organization of School Libraries, Lagos, 17—21 July, 1978.

"Writing for children: the Nigerian challenge". A paper presented at the Seminar of the Department of Library Studies, University of Ibadan, 31 May, 1984.

Chapter 17

Rosina Umelo and Nigerian Juvenalia

Helen Chukwuma

Rosina Umelo, a British married to a Nigerian, and a mother of six children, has distinguished herself as a novelist in this rapidly flourishing writing tradition. Juvenalia is one of the attendant features of a growing cultural nationalism where attention is turned to the formation of a reading culture among the youth. Prior to 1970, it was usual to find our youths interested only in reading for examinations and prescribed book were drawn from the British literary canon, Charles Dickens, Emily Bronte, George Elliot and William Shakespeare. Increasingly, such reading was found culturally vacuous and there was the crying need to relate what our youths read to their known world and reality.

Further, writing relevant books and making them available was one thing, but getting a ready reading public was another. Chinua Achebe's novel *Things Fall Apart* (1957) broke grounds in its cultural theme, style and language but it was not till the late sixties that it got the publicity and subsequent readership that it deserved. This novel proved the Nigerian creative capacity and Achebe followed up that novel with others all fresh, striking, popular and contemporary. Other writers followed in quick succession: Elechi Amadi, Flora Nwapa, Onuora Nzekwu, John Munonye and others. The novel galloped on, and as usual was dominated by male writers.

It was in the seventies that female writers burst into the field of writing and names of Buchi Emecheta, Mabel Segun, Ifeoma Okoye, Helen Ovbiagele, Adaora Lily Ulasi, joined that of Flora Nwapa in the female novelists scenario. But it is in Juvenalia that female writers' impact became obvious in the eighties. Flora Nwapa set up a series in Flora Books for children's stories. Practically every Nigerian female novelist writes a couple of children's books for lesson or leisure.[1] Children's books are to female writers what the short story is to African writers in general, an experimental genre.

In Rosina Umelo, Juvenalia was to find a profound and committed practitioner giving it the focus and seriousness it deserves. She found a ready outlet in Macmillan Pacesetter series under which she published *Felicia* (1978); *Finger of Suspicion* (1984); *Something to Hide* (1986). She also has a book of short stories, *The Man Who ate the Money* by University Press, Ibadan (1979). Most of the stories in this volume are award-winning both in Nigeria and in Britain in the nineteen sixties and severties.[2] Certainly, Umelo has distinguished herself in fiction. It will be worthwhile to consider her contribution in this regard.

Macmillan Publishers describe the Pacesetter series as dealing "with contemporary issues and problems in a way that is particularly designed to interest young adults". This age-group is the adolescent, restless, probing, protected and dependent on family. Most are still at school and they are characterized by their quest for their true selves and what they really want. This is a period of transition to adulthood and Umelo's stories depict that one event or experience that launches them into the adult world of decisions and responsibility.

Her characters are invariably young girls all placed in a home environment with varying degrees of home comfort and acceptability. Felicia is the first child of her parents and when we encounter her, she had lost her father, forced out of school to work in a hospital owing to the civil war situation. She was coming home to her poor widowed mother at the end of the war but it was not a happy homecoming for she was pregnant. The focus of the book is on the conflict which ensues because of Felicia's refusal to name the father of the child she is carrying. All the socio-cultural norms are called into question, the expectation of a mother from her daughter, the responsibility of a daughter to her immediate and extended family especially one on whom much money had been expended for her education and welfare. She was thus a failure and a great source of distress and disgrace to herself and her family. Her mother laments:

> "all through these years I prayed you would reach a good standard, marry a man who would be good to you and look after his in-laws and give you children you would be proud of in your turn. And see me now, all my hopes ended. All these years are wasted, all the miles I walked are in vain. Every penny I worked for was thrown away, you have come back like a harlot to bear a bastard and bring me shame after all my prayers and hopes for you." (p.42).

The people questioned the wisdom of educating a girl if all it yielded was shame. Umelo intensified this conflict by Felicia's silence and her refusal to name her lover. Traditional social pressure was brought on her, dispraise songs were made on her, exposing her to much ridicule and gossip. Felicia reacted by staying indoors. It was her mother who took the brunt of the exposure and she suffered under its weight. Felicia had her baby son in her cousin's house in the city, an appropriate environment for cover. The cover was short-lived and the news of her past filtered to the city. Felicia's secret was eventually out, the father of her son was a young bookish undergruduate who enlisted in the army and was tragically killed in the last days of the civil war. He had promised to marry her at the end of the war.

Umelo used the Nigerian-Biafran war as background for this story. In the unfolding of the story which basically deals with a teenage girl's problem of motherhood outside marriage, Umelo had the opportunity to introduce the physical and psychological trauma of the war: the destruction of life and property, the destabilization of family life and the closure of schools and dislocation of jobs. Umelo showed clearly that the fatalism that enveloped the people's minds especially the youth who felt completely deprived, was responsible' for the intimate relationship that all too soon bound young couples. And to a large extent the untimely death of Obioma validated life's fleeting transitoriness and made in consequence the illegitimate union of he and Felicia almost commendable. His people had to claim the young son Nkem to locate him among his kindred as the legacy bequeathed to them by their dead son Obioma through Felicia. Obioma was only one of such grave casualties of the civil war.

The cultural bond of the extended family was much exposed especially in the extended family's role as the arbiters of the welfare of members of the family. Umelo dwelt on this aspect of family anchorage. Thus at the death of her husband, Felicia's mother relied entirely on her late husband's relatives as if she had no family of her own. Felicia's fees were paid by them and they were sought in any matter of any consequence. But significantly the same members of the extended family allowed Felicia's mother to grope in her ignorance of the infamy of Felicia's pregnancy. Thus she was the last to know. This is a failure to realize in the traditional set-up the limitations of relationships. The degree of sanguinity is what divides, albeit subtly, the nucleus family and the larger family unit. This fact was not recognized and practised; in Felicia it was as if the death of the father, his entire family was subsumed in the larger family set-up. The point really is that it need not be so. It was the sheer moral strength of Felicia that made her withstand with rude stubbornness the concerted effort of all family members to push her to the sexual exploitation of Mamma Joy, the brothel-keeper from Lagos. Her mother melted with the lot leaving Felicia to fight alone and she won over the family.

Nucleus family subsumption was completely under control in *Finger of Suspicion* where Pa Agu knew when his own nucleus family interest must be safeguarded. This novel is built on the fast-gaining belief in ritual murder for the gained advantage of progress and financial success. Thus when Caro, the teenage househelp of the Agus and a relation of Mr Agu who goes to a typing school on part-time basis, disappeared, the neighbours assumed matter-of-factly that the Agus had sacrificed her for their progress. Coincidentally, soon after Caro's disappearence, Mrs Agu successfully nursed a pregnancy to term, she who hitherto had several miscarriages. Further, Mr Agu annually side-tracked for promotion by his immediate boss suddenly attracted the doting attention of the superior boss on the information that his bock *Effective Management of Junior Staff* had been accepted for publication. Agu was thus summarily promoted to the grave discomfiture of Mr Polycarp. The Agus' good fortune poured on in an endless stream in their private business partnership venture, *House enterprises,* and their eventual change of residence from Suru-lere to Victoria Island and the crown fortune of Agu starting a bungalow in his hometown. Jealousy, ill-will and suspicion engulfed their co-tenant Mama Ngozi who blurted out the accusation:

> "What did you take to kill the big man at your office? What did you take to get his job when there were others before you? What did you take to get your wife a belly? Wasn't it the head of a person? --- Where is Caro? Bring her back here. Let us all see her alive." (p.63).

The story develops on the conflict and its resolution, of finding Caro and disproving the allegation. The conflict was taken to the village where Agu's family rallied round their son against members of Caro's family. He was assured, "We shall escort you there and support whatever story you decide to tell them," (p.47). Further, Pa Agu feared for the safety of his son and had to send a pot of concoction as a form of protection for him.

The fingers of suspicion were two: the major one was that motivated by Caro's disappearance, the other one was that encountered in the office in the persons of first Mr Hadley Chase who was hounded out of office by blackmail and suspicion and second, Mr Polycarp who suspected even his own shadow and so left on his own accord. In these instances, Umelo introduced the motif of detective amateurism in the roles of husband and wife, Mr and Mrs Agu. Both went on a detective trail to clear their names of suspicion of murder and duplicity. Here, too, as in *Felicia,* Umelo prolongs suspense to almost the end of the novel. At last when suspense breaks it is not convincing but is really an anti-climax. Caro simply ran away with her boyfriend known to her parents.

Something to Hide is a bit more ambitious in the handling of characters. It features less movement of characters in travel activity. Rather, it focuses on behaviour motivations, much mental activity in scheming and planning. It shows the adolsescent problem of self-assertion in an adult world of rules, cohesion and expectation. The story is about Rachel, a typist in a secondary school who keeps house for her uncle and his wife and steal out time to work privately for extra money that will help see her through college.She had to suffer for a mistaken identity of her flighty but beautiful cousin, Helen, who left school to attend a disco party with her boy-friend. The evening of fun was cut short by her hit-and-run boy-friend driving his father's second-hand Mercedes Benz car, and had accidentally hit a motor cyclist at a bend. The incident would have continued to be kept a secret but for the betraying bright American dress of Rachel which Helen borrowed without permission. Bwana Mwakeli's wife had recognized the dress on the girl who came out of her husband's Mercedes car and had gone on to accuse Rachel publicly of having an affair with her husband. Rachel was abysmally maligned, and Helen, completely heartbroken and morally weak, was unable to own up to her guilt. Rachel accepted the role of martyr but went on again on that amateur detective spree to exonerate the guilt of her cousin and clear her own name. She succeeded after a protracted chase, multiple accusations, heartache, and loss of her boy-friend, Nwasi.

At the end of the novel, the girls had come off as mature, confident beings, with courage. The metamorphosis was more evident in Helen who acquired a new strength of character and moral purpose. Rachel on the other hand was further appreciated in the light of her true worth. And correspondingly she had shed the egoistical Nwasi for the more perceptive, tolerant and trusting Jacob.

The characters of Caro in *Finger of Suspicion* and Rachel in *Something to Hide* share the common feature of being someone else's child. This fact seems to colour all their dealings with members of the nucleus family to whom they were attached. Rachel longed for the educational privilege Helen enjoyed. Mrs Bwika, Helen's mother groaned about the rigours of bringing up somebody else's child. With regard to the accusation of Rachel she decided thus:

> Her husband would have to hear it all and investigate for himself. After all, Rachel was his own brother's daughter. Really another person's child was a great responsibility. (p.9).

This underlies the extended family structure though Umelo stops short of presenting the foster-mother image, that stereotype of wickedness. Obviously, that was not the author's concern.

The high moral stance of the writer is clear from reading these three books. The young reader's character is moulded; he is taught through the example of others that truth prevails, that life has a serious purpose which must be pursued rigorously. It is significant that in these stories, the youths are helped by their mates in their journey to self-realization and adulthood. The experiences are theirs and the mistakes are also theirs. The youths are taught to learn from their mistakes. They solve their problems by their own intelligence and surmises. Full of energy, they work fast and learn fast with little or no help from the adults. Rather, the adults themselves cause the complications by accusing the youths falsely and allowing themselves the wasteful indulgence of gossip. *In Finger of Suspicion,* Rachel, the young typist, was the topic of discussion and gossip among the teaching staff of the college, most of whom were married women.

Umelo corrects without pedantic preaching, and the significance of her success is that she points to the self as housing the ideal, and shouts the possibility of harnessing this ideal with a little more effort. She believes in the individual even at the risk of romanticizing. Even the woman of leisure, Mamma Joy, resorted to harlotry as an alternative to the life of a barren wife in a polygamous set-up. With her materialism she exhibited some charity to Felicia during her period of need; thus showing a human face.

Umelo's book of short stories, *The Man Who ate the Money* spans different years of Nigeria's socio-cultural life, from the village to the city and the faraway arena of Britain. In these setting, Umelo pitches characters in the conflict of daily living and experience. Her concern in this volume as in the others is the individual, one man juxtaposed on his society with his peculiar individual's conflict which he battles to solve himself but which he must first articulate to his kindred for advice and support. In the final analysis the resolution of the conflict lies with him. So it was with Okereke in the title story. He was the "man who ate the money." Okereke loved handling money but mishandled the people's tax money which he was at pains to return. With a little prodding he had to reverse his decision of not selling part of his landed property.

In "Uche's wife," similarly, Uche's problem is paternity of female issues only. His problem was compounded further by his being the only son of his parents and so under pressure to have an heir. He lived with his problem until he decided to solve it himself by marrying an attractive divorcee with three sons. Uzodimma came in as Uche's second wife only to bear him a daughter. The irony was complete when the first wife Chinyere bore him a son a few months later.

Obioma was plagued with a mad wife whose madness surfaced at ordered intervals. He suffered in silence and his story was made known only when the situation could not be helped. This information to his sister sets off the story of "The Mad Woman". Again, here, as in *Felicia,* and "The Businessmen", the war background and setting give an impetus to the story.

"The Golden fleece in Islington" is set in England and shows the great conflict between expectation and reality. Stephen who goes in search of the golden fleece in Islington was to realize that this venture elevated him to the realm of Midas with the golden touch who turned everything to gold. His people at home showed utter dependence on him as the family provider hardly realizing that Stephen was a poor student who lived off his part-time wages. For Stephen there just was not enough money to go round. He had the tantalizing option of Amos who completely severed communication with home people. Stephen had to educate the home people who "must realise they were quoting the wrong legend when they sent their sons abroad to seek the Golden fleece. However mighty that ram had been its precious fleece could never cover all those who looked for shelter" (p.4). In the final analysis therefore, the individual holds the key to the solution of his problems.

Umelo addresses herself to contemporary social issues which makes dating her stories easy. Stories with the war background are pointed to the post 1967–70 war years. The big market phenomenon and its attendant myths are portrayed in "Brief Visit to a Wonderful Place." In "Portobello," the reader can contrast a British market with its Nigerian counterpart as depicted in "Brief Visit to a Wonderful Place." She gives an admirable insight into village life with its peace and tranquility marked with poverty. But it is in her successful probing and baring of the mind of her characters that she excels. This is better seen in the adolescents: Helen, Rachel and Felicia.

Umelo's narrative technique of delaying the climax makes the stories to drag especially in the novels. Of account too is her custom of introducing foreign words into dialogue and narrative without translations. The reader is left to guess the meaning from the context or simply to ignore the words. What is a *matatu* or indeed *manamba*? Names of towns mentioned in the novel *Something to Hide* suggest that the language is East African. In other two novels, *Felicia* and *The Finger of Suspicion,* proverbs were used in translation and though the contexts were apt, yet something of the original appeal was lost. She sometimes gives a transliteration from Igbo as in this sentence "My hand is not there" meaning non-involvement. Reminiscent for its quaintness are the expressions "Okafor suddenly stopped and slapped his thigh" (p.21) a gesture of remembrance or dismay, an Igbo habit for men similar to the clicking of fingers or a long low whistle. And also the quaint expression of "The Man who ate the money" which is a transliteration from Igbo. Umelo finds herself this linguistic cobweb from which she never fully disentangles herself.

She succeeds in her use of irony, introducing it in the twists at the end of the stories. "The Business Man" has a tight structure with a cyclic twist of events and nemesis catches up with the lazy conniving businessman with the telling name Clandestine. In "Uche's Wife," Umelo through irony ridicules the situation of over-emphasis on male issues. It is the irony of fate that providence gives sons to one woman and daughters to another and then reverses the pattern when man expects the usual.

Umelo's major contribution lies in her themes and her readership, which, in Oladele Taiwo's mind, are part of the "readership promotion campaigns initiated by several African governments and to make available reading materials appropriate to age, circumstance and level of education."[3] Future work may revolve on a comparative analysis on works of fiction that cater for the interests of the young.

1. The list includes Flora Nwapa, Mabel Segun, Helen Ovbiagele, Theresa Meniru, Martina Nwakoby, Ifeoma Okoye.

2. Awards include "The Nigerian Broadcasting Corporation Short Story Competition" in 1972, 1974; "The Cheltenham Literary Festival" 1973; "British Broadcasting Corporation Short Story Competition" 1966. For full details see "Acknowledgements" *The Man Who Ate the Money*, 1979.

3. Oladele Taiwo, *Female Novelists of Modern African* Macmillan Publishers, 1984, p.16.

ROSINA UMELO

Born in Cheshire, England of British Parentage. Became a Nigerian citizen in 1971. Attended Bedford College, University of London and obtained B.A. Honours, Latin with Greek, in 1953. She was Education Officer, Eastern Region/East Central State, Queen's School Enugu, 1964—1975, and Principal, St. Catherine's, Nkwerre, Imo

State, 1975–1978. Was Editor, Macmillan Nigeria Publishers 1979–1987. Married with six children.

Publications

Prose and Poetry Unseen for Certificate Literature in English. London: Macmillan, 1976.
Felicia (Pacesetter). Macmillan Education, 1978.
The Man Who Ate the Money (Short Stories). OUP, 1978.
A Poetry Anthology for Junior Secondary Schools. London: Macmillan Education, 1978.
School Certificate Revision Course: English Language, 1980. (co-authored with A. I. Nwosu)
Finger of Suspicion (Pacesetter). Macmillan Education, 1984.
Something to Hide (Pacesetter). Forthcoming.

Reviews

Finger of Suspicion. Reviewed in *The Guardian* (Lagos) 21 April, 1986, p.11.
Reviewer Dili Ezughah.

Others

"A World of Our Own". Autobiographical memoir of the Nigerian Civil War (Unpublished).

Chapter 18

The Works of Rosemary Uwemedimo: A Critical Review

Chidi Ikonne

The first and, often, only book that comes to mind when Rosemary Uwemedimo's name is mentioned is *Akpan and the Smugglers*. This work, however, is not Uwemedimo's only book. First published in 1965, it is not, in fact, her first book. Rosemary Uwemedimo's other Publications include *Mammy-Wagon Marriage* (1961); *Boma and His Friend; New Nation English* (1969) which she co-authored with Anita Pincas and Bruce Pattison; *English Tests for Upper Primary Classes* (1971); and *English Tests for Common Entrance Classes in the Caribbean* (1972). *Akpan and the Smugglers,* a children's book, is nevertheless, her most widely read work. Its counterpart, *Boma and His Friends* is extremely difficult to come by.

As can be seen from above list, *Mammy-Wagon Marriage* (1961) is Rosemary Uwemedimo's first *book-length* publication. The emphasis on "book-length" is deliberate because Rosemary Uwemedimo, who was, more or less, a freelance journalist, had contributed articles to some Nigerian newspapers before the publication of her book *Mammy-Wagon Marriage* in 1961. Essentially autobiographical, this 238-page book is an account of what promises to be a successful miscegenation. It describes not only how Rosemary, a young white student, met Vincent Uwemedimo, a Nigerian Law Student, in London and got married to him in 1955, but also her journey to Nigeria with her husband, her initial impression of Nigeria and its people and her gradual assimilation of Nigerian lifestyle. The title of the book reflects a feature of this lifestyle as much as it symbolises a medley of uncertainties of an inter-racial marriage. Echoed and intensified by chapter titles, real mottos printed on real mammy-wagons which the author had observed, it strives to enhance the unity of the book.

Rosemary Uwemedimo's intention in *Mammy-Wagon Marriage,* as in all her stories, is didactic. Wondering why she began her acquaintanceship with Vincent, she confesses: "The pros and cons of inter-racial marriage never... passed through my mind ... I certainly had no grand ideals about breaking down the colour bar" (p. 18).[1] Yet *Mammy-Wagon Marriage* aims among other things, to tell "the truth" (p.211) about inter-racial marriages and thereby dispel the erroneous notions about miscegenation as embodied in novels that deal with the theme of the tragic mulatto; and to explain to European women, who want to come to Nigeria, what to expect. Witness, for instance, the information about the problem of 'hairdressing'. "Skilled dressers of African hair there are in abundance, who will spend hours patiently combing, straightening, greasing and braiding the thick, tightly curled black locks of Nigerian women, and many and elaborate are the native coiffures ... Unfortunately the technique of styling European hair is quite different, and it is useless for an English girl to summon a native hairdresser to deal with her unruly mop (p.216)".

Unlike *Akpan and the Smugglers* and *Boma and His Friends* which are mainly for a young Nigerian audience, *Mammy-Wagon Marriage* is therefore, directed almost exclusively at an adult non-African, European and American audience. As a matter of fact, Rosemary Uwemedimo herself almost says as much at different stages of her account; for instance, when she addresses her audience direct about Nigerian servants: "You have probably encountered the blase and cynical ex-colonial-type wife with her languid 'My dear, *all*[2] African servants are just born thieves', together with the staccato 'Damn' rogues, the lot of them! of her brisk empire-builder husband. How much truth is there in this? The fact is that it is all a matter of degree (p.75)". The reader also has a clue to the nature of the author's audience when, after discussing in great detail Nigerian food, she declares: "Because I believe it is interesting to most people in England I have meandered on about food for some time." (p.228).

All these point to one fact: Rosemary Uwemedimo has no doubt as to the target of her book. It is, probably, because of this that she incorporates in her otherwise original and refreshing work, which seeks to correct some wrong ideas about the black man, some of the most hackneyed features of the image of the black race in the mind of the whiteman. Examples of this stereotyping include not only such parenthetical comments as "servants are 'boys' whether they are sixteen or sixty" (p.73) and the almost endless portrayal of Africans as noisy, but also the equation of the African's knowledge of the English language with his intelligence. Thus, she describes as "a watchman who had *little brains*[3] and less English" (p. 145) a man she got on the phone when she rang up the Electricity Corporation to find out why there was no light in her house. She goes on: "What a maddening situation! Very slowly, I repeated my remarks until general sense of what I had to say penetrated the *rudimentary brain*[4] at the other end" (p.146). Witness also what she says about the African's attitude towards time: The average African ... lives completely in the present, and does not care about what is going to happen, so long as he is happy *now* ... "Sufficient unto the day, etc' is certainly the general principle for life here." (pp.166—7).[5]

Be that as it may, *Mammy-Wagon Marriage* sparkles with irresistible humour and vivid descriptions of well-observed objects and events. A reader can thus feel like a participant in the author's drama with a cockroach on p.149:

> Sometimes I am in my bedroom at night, hoping to disrobe in undisturbed peace, when I become aware that my privacy has been invaded by a miniature "Thing from Outer Space', radiating evil intent from every glossy-brown scale of its two-inch-long, armour-plated body. It glares at me from the middle of the carpet, and I am hypnotized by the waving antennae of its domed head, poked melevolently forward. Through in torment at the thought that it might run over my bare feet, I screw my courage to the sticking-point, stealthily slide off a slipper and nerve myself to strike. As if conscious of my insecticidal purpose, the loathsome object is suddenly galvanized into action and scuttles at lightning speed towards the sanctuary of my bed. With a final spurt of desperation, I hurl my footgear at its retreating back and, if fortune smiles up me, I score a bull's eye and the viscous white entrails of the pest are spattered upon my carpet. But they are so tenacious of life that their horny legs go on kicking feebly for a seeming eternity after their vital organs have been reduced to pulp.

Uwemedimo's perception of pidgin is certainly sub-standard as evidenced by her transcription of her conversation with the watchman at the Electric Corporation (pp.145-6). Yet *Mammy-Wagon Marriage* is well written in good simple English. And this is not surprising. Rosemary Uwemedimo is not only English: she is an author of textbooks that seek to teach the English language.

Her *English Tests for Upper Primary Classes,* a work book, which "consists of thirty sets of exercises and two specimen test papers of the standard expected in the First School Leaving Certificate Examination and in most secondary school examinations", (Preface) is fairly popular - especially in the Cross River State. One of its most interesting features is the inclusion of stories solidly grounded on Nigerian history and cultures. Unfortunately, this cannot be said of her contributions to *New Nation English:* chapters 9, 13, 14, 15, 16, 17 and 18. All these, except chapter 13 "An Observant Boy", which deals with an incident easily observable in Nigeria, are old European tales retold in simple English to suit upper primary and lower Secondary school pupils. Each story is followed by a set of questions to test the pupils' comprehension and develop their linguistic power.

But as educative as the exercises are, the content and methodology of *New Nation English* do not adequately take its young Nigerian audience into consideration. This is, probably, why it has not, since its publication in 1969, found a secure place in Nigerian schools, quite unlike *Akpan and the Smugglers*.

Set in the Calabar of late fifties and early sixties, Rosemary Uwemedimo's second book tells the story of a fourteen-year-old boy, Akpan Bassey, who engages in dangerous adventures to secure hard evidence which will enable him to bring about the release of his father who has been unjustly arrested.

In spite of his poverty, Bassey, a fisherman, "father of three hungry children" (p.7),[6] and husband of an unfeeling nagging wife, had not only turned down an attractive, even if criminal, offer from the controller of smugglers (who was simply known as the master) but also threatened to report him and his gang to the police. Unfortunately for him, before he could inform against them, the Master had already planted incriminating evidence (four cartons of contraband cigarettes and a crate of whisky) on him through a fisherman, Ita, his (Bassey's) wife's uncle. Akpan's efforts, therefore, are geared towards "find[ing] out who The Master is, and then get proof that papa is innocent" (p.27) - a feat which he completely achieves in the last chapter of the 75-page book.

The story, consequently, is fairly suspenseful, its brevity and the simplicity of its plot, which make it more a short story than a novel, notwithstanding. As a piece of prose, the story is well written. Its language is as direct and clear as its style is uncomplicated and fluent. Uwemedimo's attempt at pidgin is, once again, sub-standard. Witness the following utterances:

> It be crime to travel (p.42)
> Sir no go give me dash-o? (p.45).

But this attempt is so infrequent that it almost requires special attention to notice its existence. It does not, therefore, detract much from the effectiveness of Uwemedimo's style.

Her conceptualization and treatment of her characters are another matter. Imposed upon, rather than growing out of the plot, the characters are often at variance with their roles. Akpan, the central character of the story is no exception. At fourteen, he is rather too young and inexperienced for his assignment. He is, thus, guided in his unbelievable exploits by luck (a word which recurs in the text) equal to *deus ex machina*. For example, easily gaining access into the Customs Wharf, he goes into a ship and discovers, almost immediately, a clue to the personality of the Master: Mr Peter Samuel, a prominent building contractor. When locked up in a small store by the master-smuggler, he finds "a large nail" (p.59) to help him in his escape. "The shutter [of the window of his prison] itself was firmly secured, but the frame was definitely loose." (p.60) The author herself seems uneasy here. She tries an explanation which, however, cannot possibly work for an adult. "Yes that was the explanation. The mason must have tried to economise here by using too much sand and so the cement was now crumbling away. Mr Samuel had made a bad mistake when he chose this room as Akpan's prison!". (pp.61—62).

The Superintendent is definitely right when, at the end of the story, he congratulates Akpan on his prowess and says: "Akpan Bassey . . . You have shown unusual bravery and intelligence" (p.74).

In spite (is it not really because?) of this supernatural atmosphere which pervades the story, *Akpan and the Smugglers* is and will continue to be, at least for some time, a popular story among children.

REFERENCES

1. All pages of references are to Rosemary Uwemedimo, *Mammy-Wagon Marriage*, (London: Hurst & Blackett Ltd., 1961).
2. Emphasis in the original.
3. Emphasis added.
4. Emphasis in the original.
5. All page references are to Rosemary Uwemedimo, *Akpan and the Smugglers*, (Ibadan: African University Press, 1965).

ROSEMARY IRENE UWEMEDIMO

Born in London, England on the 10 April, 1933, *nee* Howard. A Nigerian by marriage. Attended Bury Grammar School for Girls, Bury, Lanes, U.K.; Bedford College, Regents Park, University of London and Institute of Education, Senate House, University of London where she obtained a B.A. Honours — Classics (1st Class Honours) and a Diploma in Education with Distinction in practical teaching. Taught in many educational institutions including Durrington Middle School, West Sussex, Davison Secondary School, Worthing, West Sussex; St Gregory's College, Lagos; Holy Child Secondary School, Calabar. Headmistress/Founder, Calabar Preparatory School, Calabar. Currently the Principal/Proprietor, Hillside International School, Calabar. Married with four sons.

Publications

Boma and His friends A.U.P.
Mammy-Wagon Marriage, Hurst and Blackett, 1961
Akpan and the Smugglers, A.U.P., 1971
English Tests for Upper Primary Classes. Nelson, 1971
New Nation English Book 6. Nelson (1969) Co-authored with Aniti Pincas and Bruce Pattison)
English Test for Common Entrance Classes in the Caribbean. (Nelson, 1972 (Co-authored with Wilfred Ramkerysingh).

GRACE N.A. OSIFO

Nee Ukala was born in Mbiri, Ika Local Government Area, Bendel State, to Godwin and Beatrice Ukala on 19 April, 1946. Attended C.M.S. School, Mbiri, 1958–1959; Anglican Girl's Grammar School, Ughelli, 1960–1964; University of Ibadan 1967–1970 and obtained B.A. (Hons) English. Obtained a post-graduate Diploma in Education from the University of London in 1977 and holds a Master's Degree in Education (Guidance and Counselling.), University of Benin, Benin City. Taught in Auchi Polytechnic, School of Business Studies, Benin City, 1974–1977, Vice Principal at Idia College, Benin City, 1977–1979; Vice Principal, Anglican Women Teachers' College, Benin City 1980–1981; Principal, Edo College III Benin City, 1981. Married with five children to Eddy Ehi Osifo. Currently the Principal of Emotan College, Benin City, Nigeria.

Publications

Dramas of Love and Marriage, a collection of Three Plays, Enugu: Nwamife, 1978.
English Language Basics. Benin City: Idodo Umeh, 1980
Dizzy Angel, Ibadan: University Press, 1985
Seven Poems in *New Nigerian Verses.* Ibadan, University Press, 1985
"The End is a Beginning" in (a poem), *Ibadan Literature Review,* 1, 1969, p.26

INDEX